I0813453

Introduction to the Zohar
The Wisdom of Truth

Rabbi Yehuda Leib Ashlag

Introduction to the
ZOHAR
The Wisdom of Truth

TRANSLATED BY

Yoel Finkelman

Share
Maggid Books

Introduction to the Zohar: The Wisdom of Truth

First Edition, 2025

Maggid Books
An imprint of Koren Publishers Jerusalem Ltd.

POB 8531, New Milford, CT 06776-8531, USA
& POB 4044, Jerusalem 9104001, Israel
www.korenpub.com

English translation of *Introduction to the Zohar* by Yoel Finkelman.

The Hebrew text is courtesy of Makhon Zohar HaSulam
HeḤadash – המאמר באדיבות מכון זוהר הסולם החדש

The publication of this book was made possible
through the generous support of *The Jewish Book Trust.*

ISBN 978-1-59264-663-0, *hardcover*

Printed and bound in the United States

"The Zohar will bring them out of exile in mercy" (Zohar, Naso)

יהו ספר הזוהר יפקון ביה מן גלותא ברחמי (זוהר, נשא)

Dedicated in honor of our dear spouses, children, and families.
With awe and respect to our teachers, who
brought us on this important journey.
In appreciation of Sefaria, who connected us to Koren
and who continue to share Torah with the world.

Share

Contents

Foreword

Benji Levy

In the beginning, the infinite light of God was all that existed. Everything was, by definition, perfect. Except it wasn't for God, for an element of the ultimate perfection always strives for more.[1] God wanted to give, which required a recipient with needs and deficiencies. Therefore, He had to make space for imperfection so that He could bestow goodness.[2] It seems counterintuitive for those who seek wholeness and holiness, but it is this deficiency that animates the possibility of life itself. There are terrible side effects of this philosophical approach, such as tragedy and loss. And yet, the soul-searching born at these difficult moments can allow us to build something new.[3] Just as bending one's knees allows one

1. See for example R. Kook, *Shemoneh Kevatzim* 8:43.
2. For this understanding of *tzimtzum* as revealing hidden deficiency, see, for example, R. Azriel of Gerona's *Esser Sefirot BaDerekh She'ala VeTeshuva*; the accompanying preface printed in R. Moshe Schatz's *Tarshish Shoham VeYishpeh* (Jerusalem, 2023); the Arizal's explanation of *tzimtzum* in R. Hayim Vital, *Etz Ḥayim* 1:1; *Mevo Shearim* 1:1:1; the writings of the *Leshem Shevo VeAḥlama: Hakdamot UShearim* (Jerusalem: Barzani), *shaar heh*, ch. 1, p. 82; *Sefer HaKlalim* (Barzani), *klal yud*, ch. 1, p. 113. This idea is fully developed in the writings of R. Moshe Chaim Luzzatto (the Ramḥal), who serves as a foundation for the teachings of R. Ashlag; see, for example, *Klaḥ Pitḥei Ḥokhma* (Jerusalem: Spinner edition, 2012), *petaḥ* 24. *Klalim Rishonim* (Spinner edition), *klal* 1–4.
3. The notion of descent for the sake of an ascent (*yerida letzorekh aliya*) is central in many places across the writings of Kabbala and *Ḥasidut*; see for example *Keter Shem Tov* (New York: Kehot, 2004), nos. 26, 96, and 136. This is true not only from

to jump higher, the descent into darkness can allow for a new and even higher ascent that was previously unattainable. This truth reverberates across the expanse of Jewish history.

While it seems that absence is the opposite of growth, approaching this element of imperfection in the right way can actually drive growth. The first human being was created with desires, deficiencies, and dependencies, yet these were to be filled towards a wholeness beyond oneself.[4] Adam and Eve were exiled out of the Garden of Eden, and at the same time this catalyzed their mission to illuminate the world. The matriarchs, Sarah, Rebecca, and Rachel, experienced the hopelessness of infertility and came to cherish the profundity of possibility and life itself.[5] A single family unit was enslaved in Egypt and emerged as the Israelite nation – returning to its homeland and building a society founded on compassion and care for those in need. The holy Temples were destroyed, and it was from these ruins that the grandeur and potency of the Oral Law came forth.[6] R. Shimon bar Yoḥai was forced into the darkness of a cave,[7] and emerged with the book of splendor and illumination, the Zohar.

As students of history, we can see the tremendous strength that can be incubated from within the crucible of struggle. The attainment of this strength takes place through the descent, a process that often brings one face to face with apparent emptiness. This sense of emptiness, however, is not a flaw but rather a feature of how and why God created the world.[8] While this happens on a macro level across the universe, "each

---

a psychological standpoint, but can be understood as fundamentally a part of the world's makeup; for example, whereby the purification of the vessels occurs through their shattering, see R. Chaim Vital, Etz *Ḥayim* (Barzani) 11:5; cf. R. Shlomo Elyashiv's *Leshem Shevo VeAḥlama: Drushei Olam HaTohu* (Barzani, 2004) in *Maamar Klali*, pp. 9–16.

4. See R. Moshe Chaim Luzzatto, *Drush HaKivui* printed in *Otzrot HaRamḥal* (Spinner edition, 2002), p. 246.
5. See Yevamot 64a.
6. The direct association between the destruction of the Temples, the disappearance of prophecy, and the development of the Oral Law is a theme developed by R. Tzadok HaKohen of Lublin throughout his many writings; see for example *Resisei Layla* (Jerusalem: Machon Har Bracha, 2004), pp. 11–21, 99, 266–271.
7. See Shabbat 33b.
8. For R. Ashlag, the "desire-to-receive" is rooted in the *tzimtzum* not by virtue of a lack

person is a world unto themselves."[9] Taking an honest look at our own vulnerability, it is not difficult to uncover the common thread of loss and hardship, and at the same time, to identify the way that it can give birth to hope and strength.[10]

And so, as the World Wars and the Holocaust thrust society into doubt and turmoil, a new spiritual revolution was brewing.[11] R. Yehuda Leib Halevy Ashlag had a vision to build a ladder (*sulam*) that would elevate beyond confusion and allow us to connect with and become more than our limited persona. He saw a future where the Zohar, the teachings of the Arizal, and other fundamental mystical sources could be a guide toward the ideal sense of self, the ideal family, and even the ideal society. Through his radical spiritual promise, even our impure and broken parts could be transformed into tools for revealing God's plan and perfection.

R. Ashlag understood that it was precisely at this moment in history that this eternal mission became more urgent than ever: "Now I feel with all six hundred and thirteen parts of my being, that all the promises of the Zohar regarding the revelation of this wisdom at the end of days, even for the youth, were said regarding this generation."[12] The innermost teachings, *Pnimiyut HaTorah*, were entrusted to a select few for two thousand years, until our generation, when more expansive access was

---

of God's presence in the world, but by the tangible presence of lack in the world. See for example *Pri Ḥakham: Siḥot Kodesh* (Bnei Brak, 1997), pp. 64–70.

9. Sanhedrin 37a.
10. R. Mordechai Yosef Leiner of Izhbitz and others explain that each person descends down into this world to rectify a *nitzotz*, a particular point of deficiency which is the root of all their subjective experience. See for example *Mei Shiloaḥ, Parashat Bereshit* (Bnei Brak: Meishor, 1995), pp. 12–16. This is also a significant theme in the writings of R. Ashlag; see for example *Pri Ḥakham: Siḥot Kodesh*, pp. 23–40.
11. For a very similar response to uncertainty and chaos, see R. Abraham Isaac Hacohen Kook's introduction to *Reish Milin* (Jerusalem: Mosad HaRav Kook, 2006), written while he was stuck outside the Land of Israel as a result of the First World War. R. Kook explains that when the world is operating in order, then the spiritual, sensitive soul can draw its sustenance from the external parts of things. When darkness and concealment emerge, however, the sensitive soul must descend inwards to find a new source of sustenance. The soul is called inwards to find the comfort it needs.
12. *Hakdama LeḤokhmat HaKabbala*, printed in *Hakdamot HaSulam* (Bnei Brak: Makhon Ohr HaSulam, 5782), p. 249.

granted in order to heal our fragmented world.[13] He saw the Holocaust and its associated darkness as so cataclysmic that it necessitated healing through the teachings of the inner dimension, hitherto unrevealed to this extent, and explained that the proper response to radical evil was revealing radical goodness, and *Pnimiyut HaTorah* could chart a path.[14]

R. Ashlag, among others, identified our generation as the one that can merit the end of conflict and history as we know it, heralding the messianic redemption.[15] One key stepping stone lay in the fact that "the Zohar will bring them out of exile in mercy."[16] This redemption was not just for the world that contains each person, but for each person's world. The study of the Zohar empowers an individual to extract themselves, "like an ark floating within the waters of a flood, a city of refuge for one being chased."[17] This book – his introduction to the Zohar – is thus an expression of his life mission: to hasten the redemption. That means bridging from one space to another, from the reality that *is*, to the

13. The ban against revealing the secrets of Torah to the masses was all but cast to the side in times of severe concealment, when the only thing potent enough to save the Jewish people was the inner teachings. See R. Yaakov Tzemach's introduction to *Sefer Etz Ḥayim* where he discusses how this revelation is rooted in the existential need for meaning and comfort. It is this framework that gives us an insight into the various points throughout history when new levels of insight were revealed in an almost paradigm-shifting way, a theme clearly outlined in the writings of R. Tzvi Hirsch Eichenstein of Zidichov; see his *Sur MeRah VeAseh Tov* (Jerusalem: Makhon Emet, 2013), pp. 78–82, as well as the commentary of R. Tzvi Elimelech of Dinov, the *Bnei Yissacher,* printed there. R. Ashlag's perspective on the urgency of revelation may be connected to the arguments made clearly by Ramḥal in his *Adir BaMarom* (Jerusalem: Makhon HaRamḥal, 2018), pp. 38–39, regarding the suspension of the normative restrictions placed on revealing this wisdom.
14. For an astounding formulation of this, see R. Binyamin Sinkofsky, *Nishmat Yisrael, Ktavim Ḥadashim MiBaal Yad Binyamin,* compiled by Yaakov Klein (Jerusalem: Makhon Nishmat Yisrael, 5784), p. 107.
15. *Maamrei Baal HaSulam: Ḥelek Bet* (Bnei Brak, 2021), no. 231. See as well the remarkable comments of the *Leshem Shevo VeAḥlama* regarding our generation's being ripe for the revelation of the inner wisdom, in *Leshem Sefer HaBiurim* (Barzani, 2004), p. 38; *Leshem Sefer HaDeah* (Barzani, 2002), p. 157.
16. Zohar, 3:90a; see R. Daniel Frisch's *Shaarei HaZohar* (Jerusalem, 2005), ch. 4, for a full array of sources describing the connection between the Zohar and redemption.
17. R. Moshe Chaim Luzzatto's *Adir BaMarom*, pp. 22–24.

reality that *ought* to be. It means striving to become a ladder, "standing firmly on the ground with his head reaching the heavens."[18]

This great vision of R. Ashlag took time for the world to process, and its influence continues to take shape as more and more people internalize its meaning and message. According to the tradition held by R. Ashlag's students, his task was to ultimately complete the spiritual project of the saintly individuals of the past.[19] His legacy was not to shy away from paradox, but to show the wholeness which is too often concealed beneath conflict and confusion. In this sense, he is a ladder between the worlds of giving and receiving, mystics and rationalists, Hasidim and their Lithuanian counterparts, heavens and earth.

As the inaugural book of this new initiative called Share, we see this work not just as an introduction to the Zohar, but an introduction to a new expression of this goal. Just as R. Ashlag didn't only introduce the Zohar through this work but wrote a full commentary and translation, among other important teachings, Share will continue to publish, produce, and support other important works in different formats and through experiences, innovative opportunities for growth, and partnerships with others advancing this mission.

We are truly grateful for this unique opportunity. Thank you Hashem. And thank you to Hashem's partners, the visionaries and supporters, donors and friends, who drive the Share mission. Of course, this includes the amazing professional staff at Share, and in particular two of our Share scholars – R. Jeremy Tibbetts and R. Joey Rosenfeld – who were study partners and teachers in developing this foreword and much of our early educational work.

We are proud that this is the first time this type of literature is published, first digitally and then in print. For that we are grateful to our dear friends Sam Moed, Daniel Septimus, and the entire Sefaria team

18. Genesis 28:12.
19. See R. Yitzchak Meir Morgenstern's approbation to *Otiyot DiLibi* (Bnei Brak, 2012), p. 4; see as well his introduction to *Nishmat Yisrael, Ktavim Ḥadashim MiBaal Yad Binyamin*, pp. 3–11. See the comments of R. Ashlag in his Introduction to *Panim Meirot UMasbirot*, printed in *Hakdamot LeḤokhmat HaEmet* (Telzstone: Ohr Barukh Shalom, 2009), pp. 113–114, where he describes his spiritual mission as beginning where the path of the Baal Shem Tov ends, to draw down this path even further.

for making this and so many important works available to the masses. We are of course grateful to Matthew and Yehoshua Miller, true partners in every sense, who together with their tremendous team, R. Reuven Ziegler, R. David Silverstein, Tzvi Goldstein, Meira Mintz, Avichai Gamdani, Ita Olesker, Rina Ben Gal, and Tani Bayer, published this and are committed to publishing the widest range of classical Jewish texts to the highest levels of accuracy, authenticity, and design. Thank you to R. Dr. Zvi Leshem for his insightful introduction, Dr. Yoel Finkelman for his erudite translation, and, of course, R. Ashlag for revealing these illuminations.

Rabbi Dr. Benji Levy is the CEO of Share

Preface

Zvi Leshem

The hasidic kabbalist Rabbi Yehuda Leib HaLevi Ashlag (Warsaw, 1885 – Tel Aviv, 1954), who made *aliya* to Jerusalem in 1921, was undoubtedly one of the greatest and most influential kabbalists of the twentieth century. Raised in a hasidic family in Warsaw, as a young man, Rabbi Ashlag came in contact with numerous hasidic masters, most notably Rabbi Yissachar Dov Rokeach of Belz, whom he met when he was eighteen. Steeped in talmudic and kabbalistic knowledge from his youth, Rabbi Ashlag was ordained at age nineteen and served as a *dayan* on the Warsaw *beit din*. A dramatic turn in his life came in 1918, when he met a businessman who was also a profound but secret kabbalist. Rabbi Ashlag studied with him on and off for a few months until, after a night of study pertaining to the mystical interpretations of the *mikve*, the teacher passed away, having forbidden Rabbi Ashlag to reveal his identity.

Arriving in Eretz Yisrael a few years later, Rabbi Ashlag gathered around him a few close disciples with whom he would study Kabbala every night from 1:00 a.m. until 9:00 in the morning. He moved numerous times, beginning in Jerusalem's Old City, where he argued with the veteran Sephardi kabbalists of Yeshivat Beit El yeshiva (see below), and later moving to the Givat Shaul neighborhood of Jerusalem, where he served as the official neighborhood rabbi. He also spent time in Warsaw, London, Tel Aviv, and Bnei Brak, eventually settling in Tel Aviv for the last years of his life.

Rabbi Ashlag was a prolific writer, with his most notable publications being the multi-volume *Talmud Eser Sefirot* on the Lurianic writings (1937) and his magnum opus, the *HaSulam* ("The Ladder") Hebrew translation of and commentary on the Zohar (1945–1954), from which he received the appellation *Baal HaSulam* ("Master of the Ladder"). After his death, he was succeeded by his son Rabbi Baruch Shalom as *Admor* of what essentially became a small hasidic sect, which continues to this day.

The Ashlagian project should be viewed in the context of a much wider picture of the move from esotericism to exotericism and the popularization of Kabbala in the last century, in which both Rabbi Ashlag and his friend, Chief Rabbi Abraham Isaac Kook, played major roles. In the decades following Rabbi Ashlag's death, his disciples, and especially their students, split into various factions, ranging from *ḥaredi* on the right to the completely universalistic New Age "Kabbalah Centre" on the left. The latter has done much to publicize Rabbi Ashlag and his writings (especially in English and other translations) well beyond the Orthodox Jewish world that was his own spiritual milieu.

Rabbi Ashlag viewed himself as a Lurianic purist in his kabbalistic approach. In one passage, he claimed that he had "merited the soul of the holy Ari" and had received a prophetic revelation saying, "I have chosen you to be the *tzaddik* and sage for this generation in order that the crises of humanity may be healed with a lasting salvation." In a letter he penned to a disciple in 1927, he wrote, "There is nothing new here [in my teachings] at all, because everything that I wrote is already written in the writings of the Ari – this, actually is the truth... I did not add anything at all to the writings of the Ari. My intention is simply to remove stumbling blocks from those who are limping and blind."

What certainly appears to be novel in the Ashlagian system is his emphasis on the need of the individual to radically transform himself from egoism ("the desire to receive") to altruism ("the desire to give"). This point is related to his above-mentioned dispute with the kabbalists of Yeshivat Beit El in Jerusalem. His protestations notwithstanding, Rabbi Ashlag was an innovator. Rabbi Ashlag viewed the Lurianic kabbalists of Beit El as having no interest in understanding the texts they mastered and declaimed by heart. The main difference, as Rabbi Ashlag perceived it, was between the Jerusalem school's focus on textual mastery of the Lurianic corpus and his own attempt to uncover the inner meaning of the texts and how to apply them to one's spiritual life. Rabbi Ashlag felt that he arrived at the inner practical application of these texts. In his own description of the confrontation with the kabbalistic masters he found in Jerusalem, he wrote:

> When I met with the people, I clearly saw their spiritual poverty, their ignorance and their foolish ways.... Here there is no clear voice in the wisdom of the Kabbala....They just see Kabbala as a collection of words and names with no parable and its solution, only literal words.
>
> Then I met the more famous of them. These are men who spent years learning the Zohar and the writings of the Ari to the extent that they are able to recite the books of the Ari to a wondrous degree, and they are known as holy men. I asked them if they had learned with a teacher, one who had attained the inner meaning of these matters. But they replied, "God forbid! There are no inner meanings! Only the words as they are written were handed down to us...." At this point, I poured out my anger on them, because I had no more patience to be in their company.

One can, of course, question his evaluation of his opponents' approach. Beit El, at least from the time of Rabbi Shalom Sharabi (the Rashash, 1720–1777), also had a very rich ritualistic approach to prayer, focusing on the Lurianic *kavanot* that the Rashash explained and elaborated upon. The Baal Shem Tov's brother-in-law, Rabbi Gershon Kitover, arriving in Jerusalem in the 1740s, became part of Beit El, despite his hasidic approach to Kabbala and ecstatic spiritual life. Nonetheless, this is apparently not what Rabbi Ashlag perceived in his encounter with the kabbalists of Beit El. He continued on his own and revealed his own approach, in which the inner meaning of Kabbala is to train oneself in selfless altruism.

One might also argue that there is no need for such a radical dichotomy in relating to the Lurianic corpus. That is, a *peshat* approach to the texts could still lead to practical applications, and in fact it would seem that this was the case in Beit El, although the applications were apparently not in the direction that Rabbi Ashlag believed in.

It is worth noting that Rabbi Ashlag's philosophical positions may have had political overtones as well. Rumor has it that the British authorities once closed down his printing press, citing his "Communist sympathies." Perhaps not surprisingly, his brother-in-law and close disciple, Rabbi Yehuda Zvi Brandwein, served as the rabbi for the Histadrut national labor union.

All of which brings us to the *Introduction to the Zohar*. When Rabbi Ashlag published the first edition of the *Sulam* translation of and commentary on the Zohar in 1945, the first volume included three different introductions of sorts, the "Introduction" (הקדמה), the "Preface" (מבוא), and the "Opening" (פתיחה), the latter having been penned around 1942 and published in a condensed form to avoid repetition. They have subsequently been republished, although not in every printing of the *Sulam*. Most recently, they appeared in a Hebrew book, "*Hakdamot HaSulam* – Introductions of the Sulam."[1] The "Introduction" is the most basic of the three, and it also deals with the importance of the study of Kabbala and the Zohar. The "Preface" delves more deeply into Zoharic concepts, and the "Opening" even more so.

The "Introduction," ably rendered into English here by Yoel Finkelman, consists of seventy-one sections, with titles added to groups of sections by later editors. Among the topics discussed in this wide-ranging essay are the nature of the world and of human beings, the aforementioned egoistic "desire to receive" and the need to transform it into the altruistic "desire to give" (or "to influence"), the way the soul is altered during this transformation, and the soul-body relationship. Rabbi Ashlag refutes the views of "the philosophers" on these matters and explains how the kabbalistic worldview disagrees with them. He also enumerates classic kabbalistic concepts, such as the five levels of the soul, the four levels of creation (inanimate, vegetation, animal, and human), and the five "worlds" and their relation to the ten *Sefirot*, divine attributes. He stresses the importance of the study of Kabbala for all Jews and explains

1. Bnei Brak, 2019.

this as the motivation for authoring his *Talmud Eser Sefirot* on the Lurianic corpus and the *Sulam* on the Zohar.

Rabbi Ashlag explained the title of his work:

> I titled this commentary "The Ladder [*HaSulam*]," for my commentary functions like a ladder. If an attic is full of treasure, you need only a ladder to ascend, and then all of the good in the world is available to you. The ladder is not the goal in itself. If you rest on the rungs of the ladder, you will never reach the attic or achieve your goal. The same is true of my commentary on the Zohar. Words are not adequate to fully explain these infinitely deep matters. Yet, I was able in my commentary to provide a path, an introduction, for all people so that they can ascend and understand the depths of the book of Zohar itself. That is the real goal of my commentary.[2]

Elsewhere, Rabbi Ashlag reiterates the traditional view that the Zohar was authored by the *Tanna* R. Shimon bar Yoḥai and the importance of understanding the "physical" allegories in the Zohar in a non-literal manner. Rabbi Ashlag was of the opinion that since we are approaching the Messianic Redemption, permission to reveal formerly esoteric knowledge to the masses has been granted. In this regard, he writes: "By being involved in studying the Zohar and the wisdom of [kabbalistic] truth, a person can bring about the end of the exile and the complete redemption."[3] Alluding to the recent *Shoah* (Rabbi Ashlag began working on his commentary in 1943, and the first volume appeared in 1945), he states that "the redemption of Israel and its level depends upon the study of the Zohar and the internal aspects of Torah; hence, all of the destruction and the descent of Israel in our generation (may God protect us from them). Israel's success depends on the study of the Zohar and the internal aspects of Torah."[4]

2. Chapter 58.
3. Chapter 68.
4. Chapter 69.

In light of the above, Rabbi Ashlag's "Introduction" is a crucial text for several reasons. First, it is a clear restatement of basic kabbalistic principles for the reader who wishes to engage with the "inner Torah." Second, it provides us with a method for approaching the Zohar, and especially for utilizing the extremely helpful *Sulam* commentary. Last, and perhaps most uniquely, it gives us a clear window into the spiritual world of Rabbi Ashlag himself and the historical-spiritual context in which he attempted, with much success, to propagate his message. And if, along the way, we also manage to transform, at least partially, our "desire to receive" into the "desire to give," he will have empowered us to make the world just a bit of a better place.

Rabbi Dr. Zvi Leshem directed the Gershom Scholem Collection for Kabbalah and Hasidism at the National Library of Israel in Jerusalem until his retirement in 2024.

PUBLISHER'S NOTE

We note that the chapter titles, chapter summaries, headings, and summary chart on page 69 are editorial additions and do not appear in the Rabbi Ashlag's original work.

Introduction to the Zohar
The Wisdom of Truth

הקדמות לחכמת האמת - ספר הזוהר

הקדמה

שאלות וחקירות

א׳

רצוני בהקדמה זו לברר איזה דברים פשוטים לכאורה, כלומר אשר ידי הכל ממשמשות בהם והרבה דיו נשפכה בכדי לבררם, ובכל זאת עדיין לא הגענו בהם לידי ידיעה ברורה ומספקת.

שאלה א׳: מה מהותנו.
שאלה ב׳: מה תפקידנו בשלשלת המציאות הארוכה, שאנו טבעות קטנות הימנה.
שאלה ג׳: הנה כשאנו מסתכלים על עצמנו, אנו מרגישים את עצמנו מקולקלים ושפלים עד שאין כמונו לגנות – וכשאנו מסתכלים על הפועל שעשה אותנו, הרי אנו מחויבים להימצא ברום המעלות שאין כמוהו לשבח. כי הכרח הוא שמפועל השלם תצאנה פעולות שלמות.
שאלה ד׳: לפי שהשכל מחייב, הלא הוא ית׳ הטוב ומטיב שאין למעלה הימנו ית׳, ואיך ברא מלכתחילה כל כך הרבה בריות שתתענינה

Introduction

Questions and Inquiries

Rabbi Ashlag begins his introduction to the Zohar by asking a series of fundamental philosophical questions about the nature of God, the universe, and humanity. Ultimately, he believes that a picture of creation informed by Kabbala is the best framework to make sense of the questions and paradoxes that appear in the world.

1

In this introduction [to Kabbala], I would like to clarify certain ideas that might seem simple. People mention ideas, and much ink has been spilled explaining those ideas, but people do not clearly and properly understand them.

My questions are:

- What is our [human] essence?
- What is our role in this great chain of being, of which each of us is but a small link?
- When we examine ourselves, we feel that we are defective and low. There is little more despicable than we are. When we examine the Maker who made us, we ought to be superior and perfect, as a perfect Maker ought to make perfect things.
- Logic dictates that God is the Great Benefactor, and none are greater than Him. Why has He created so many creatures

ותתייסרנה בכל ימי היותן, והלא מדרך הטוב להטיב, ועל כל פנים לא להרע כל כך.

שאלה ה׳: איך אפשר שמהנצחי שאין לו ראשית ואין לו תכלית, תמשכנה בריות הוות וכלות ונפסדות.

ב׳

ובכדי לברר כל זה בשלמות צריכים אנו להקדים איזה חקירות. ולא ח״ו במקום האסור, דהיינו בעצמותו של הבורא ית׳, אשר ׳לית מחשבה תפיסא בו כלל וכלל׳ ואין לנו משום זה שום מחשבה והגה בו ית׳ – אלא במקום שהחקירה היא מצוה, דהיינו החקירה במעשיו ית׳, כמצוה לנו בתורה (דבה״י א׳ כח, ט): ״דע את אלהי אביך ועבדהו״, וכן אומר בשיר היחוד (ליום חמישי): ״ממעשיך הכרנוך״.

והנה חקירה הא׳ היא: איך יצויר לנו שהבריאה תהיה מחודשת, שפירושו דבר חדש שלא היה כלול בו ית׳ מטרם שבראו, בה בעת שברור לכל בעל עיון שאין לך דבר שלא יהיה כלול בו ית׳, וכן השכל הפשוט מחייב, כי כלום יש לך נותן מה שאין בו.

חקירה הב׳: אם תמצא לומר שמבחינת כל יכלתו ודאי הוא שיכול לברוא יש מאין, דהיינו דבר חדש שאין לו שום מציאות בו ית׳. נשאלת השאלה, מה היא מציאות הזו שיתכן להחליט עליה שאין לה שום מקום בו ית׳ אלא היא מחודשת.

חקירה הג׳: במה שאמרו המקובלים שנשמתו של אדם היא חלק אלוה ממעל, באופן שאין הפרש בינו ית׳ לבין הנשמה, אלא שהוא ית׳ ׳כל׳ והנשמה ׳חלק׳. והמשילו זה לאבן הנחצבת מההר, שאין הפרש בין האבן לבין ההר אלא שזה ׳כל׳ וזו ׳חלק׳. לפי זה יש לחקור, הא תינח אבן הנחלקת מההר, שהיא נפרדת מההר על ידי גרזן המוכן לכך ונפרד על ידו ה׳חלק׳

who suffer and experience lack during their existence? Good desires to bestow good, and certainly not to generate so much suffering.

- How is it possible that from the Eternal, which has no beginning nor end, will emanate creatures that come into being, cease to be, and are lowly?

2

To adequately explain all of this, we must initially make certain inquires. [These inquiries are] not regarding forbidden things, such as God's essence, of which we have no knowledge whatsoever and about which we can neither think nor say anything. Instead, [we should inquire] about those matters that we are commanded to study: namely, God's actions. As the Torah commands: "Know the God of your father and serve Him" (I Chr. 28:9), and as it is also stated in *Shir HaYiḥud* (for Thursday): "You [God] are known through Your actions."

The first inquiry is: How can we imagine a genuinely new creation, something created that was not already contained within God prior to Creation? After all, it is clear to anyone who investigates that there is nothing that is not already included within Him. Furthermore, it is evident that nothing can produce what is not already contained within it.

The second inquiry is: Let us grant that, as an omnipotent being, God can create *ex nihilo*, i.e., something completely new that is not already contained in any way in God. Still, we must ask: What exactly is that "something" that God could choose to create without it being already contained within Him, but is instead entirely new?

The third inquiry is: The kabbalists say that the soul of man is a part of God above, such that there is no distinction between God and the soul. God is the "whole" and the soul is "part." This is comparable to a stone hewn from a mountain, in that the only difference between the stone and the mountain is that the stone is a "part" of the "whole" mountain. We imagine a stone quarried from a mountain by an axe built for that purpose, such that the "part" is

מה׳כל׳, אבל איך יצויר זה בו ית׳ וית׳, שיפריד חלק מן עצמותו ית׳ עד שיצא מעצמותו ית׳ ויהיה ׳חלק׳ נבדל הימנו, דהיינו לנשמה, עד שיתכן להבינה רק כחלק מעצמותו ית׳.

ג׳

חקירה הד׳: כיון שמרכבת הסטרא אחרא והקליפות רחוקה מקדושתו ית׳ מהקצה אל הקצה עד שלא תצויר הרחקה כזאת – איך אפשר שתתמשך ותתהוה מהקדושה ית׳. ולא עוד אלא שקדושתו ית׳ תקיים אותה.

חקירה הה׳: ענין תחיית המתים. כיון שהגוף הוא דבר בזוי כל כך, עד שתכף מעת לידתו נידון למיתה וקבורה, ולא עוד אלא שאמרו בזוהר (עי׳ זוהר תרומה אותיות רפד, תנו) שמטרם שהגוף נרקב כולו לא תוכל הנשמה לעלות למקומה לגן עדן, כל עוד שיש איזה שיור הימנו – אם כן מהו החיוב שיחזור ויקום לתחיית המתים, וכי לא יוכל הקב״ה לענג את הנשמות בלעדו. ויותר תמוה מה שאמרו חז״ל, שעתידים המתים לקום ולהחיות במומם, כדי שלא יאמרו אחר הוא, ואח״ז ירפא את המומים שלהם (זוהר אמור אות נא). ויש להבין, מה אכפת לו להקב״ה שיאמרו אחר הוא, עד שבשביל זה הוא יחזור ויברא את המום שבהם ויוצרך לרפאותם.

חקירה הו׳: במה שאמרו ז״ל אשר האדם הוא מרכז כל המציאות, שכל העולמות העליונים ועולם הזה הגשמי וכל מלואם, לא נבראו אלא בשבילו (זוהר תזריע אות קיג), וחייבו את האדם להאמין שבשבילו נברא העולם (סנהדרין לז, א) – שלכאורה קשה להבין שבשביל האדם הקטן הזה שאינו תופס ערך של שערה בערך מציאות העולם הזה, ומכל־שכן בערך כל העולמות העליונים שאין קץ להם ולרוממותם, טרח הקב״ה לברוא כל אלו בשבילו. וכן למה לו לאדם כל זה.

separated from the "whole." But how is that possible in the case of God? How can a "part" be separated from Him? How can we think of the soul only as a part of God's essence?

3

The fourth inquiry is: The *sitra aḥra* [the "Other Side," the forces of evil] and the *kelipot* ["husks," a kabbalistic expression for negative aspects of reality] are unimaginably distant from God's sanctity. How, then, could these emerge and come into being out of God's sanctity? Could it be that God's sanctity actually exists within them?!

The fifth inquiry relates to the resurrection of the dead. The body is contemptible, and from the moment of birth it is already destined for death and burial. The Zohar even states (*Teruma* 284, 457) that the soul cannot rise to its place in the Garden of Eden before the body has completely decomposed, leaving no trace. If so, what is the purpose of the [bodily] resurrection? Could God not delight the soul without the body? There is a greater question. The Sages state that the dead will be resurrected with their bodily defects, so that no one will say that he is a different person. Afterward, God will heal those bodily defects (Zohar, *Emor* 51). Why does God care that someone might say that the [resurrected] person is someone else?! Why does God need to recreate people's defects and then heal them?

The sixth inquiry is: The Zohar (*Tazria* 40) states that man is the center of reality and that all of the upper worlds as well as all of this material world and all it contains were created for the sake of man. The Talmud states (Sanhedrin 37a) that a person must believe that the world was created for him. It seems difficult to understand that all of creation is for the sake of insignificant man, who is less than a hairsbreadth compared to the whole of existence. This becomes even more difficult to understand when man is compared to the infinite and lofty upper worlds. Why would God bother to create all of them for man? And what does man need with all of this?!

פרק א׳

הרצון לקבל

תכלית הבריאה

ד׳

ובכדי להבין כל אלו השאלות והחקירות, תחבולה האחת היא להסתכל בסוף המעשה, כלומר בתכלית הבריאה. כי אי אפשר להבין שום דבר באמצע מלאכתו אלא מסופו. וזה ברור הוא שאין לך פועל בלי תכלית. כי רק מי שאינו שפוי בדעתו תמצאהו פועל בלי תכלית.

ויודע אני שיש מתחכמים פורקי עול תורה ומצוות, שאומרים שהבורא ית׳ ברא את כל המציאות ועזב אותה לנפשה, כי מחמת האפסיות שבאלו הבריות, אינו מתאים לבורא ית׳ לרוב רוממותו להשגיח על דרכיהן הפעוטות והמגונות. אכן לא מדעת דברו זאת. כי לא יתכן להחליט על שפלותנו ואפסותנו, מטרם שנחליט שאנחנו עשינו את עצמנו ואת כל אלו הטבעים המקולקלים והמגונים שבנו. אבל בה בעת שאנו מחליטים אשר הבורא ית׳, השלם בכל השלמות, הוא בעל המלאכה שברא ותיכן את גופותנו, על כל מיני נטיות הטובות והמגונות שבהם – הרי מתחת

Part 1

The Desire to Receive

Humans appear to be lowly and materialistic. In fact, however, they are the loftiest of creatures, the very purpose of creation. God longs to provide greatness and pleasure to His creatures, but greatness and pleasure stem from overcoming weaknesses and challenges of repair. Hence, humans were created with a lowly body and materialistic drives – the desire to receive – such that those could be overcome through a process of purification.

THE PURPOSE OF CREATION

4

One strategy for answering these questions is to begin with the end – namely, the end [i.e., purpose] of creation. After all, one cannot understand anything from the middle, only from its end. Clearly, every action has a purpose, since only an insane person acts purposelessly.

I know that there are thinkers – those who reject the yoke of Torah and mitzvot – who say that the Creator created reality and then abandoned it due to the insignificance of creatures. It is inappropriate for the Creator to have providence over their insignificant and distasteful actions. This is foolish. This would be a reasonable conclusion if we [humans] had created ourselves along with all of the distasteful and defective aspects of our nature. But we have concluded that God, the most perfect of beings, is the craftsman who created and designed our bodies – with all of their positive and defective traits. A distasteful and

יד הפועל השלם לא תצא לעולם פעולה בויה ומקולקלת, וכל פעולה מעידה על טיב פועלה, ומה אשמתו של בגד מקולקל אם איזה חייט לא יוצלח תפר אותו? ע׳ כגון זה במסכת תענית (כ, א): מעשה שבא ר׳ אלעזר בר״ש וכו׳, נזדמן לו אדם אחד שהיה מכוער ביותר וכו׳. אמר לו, כמה מכוער אותו האיש וכו׳. אמר לו, לך ואמור לאומן שעשאני: כמה מכוער כלי זה שעשית וכו׳, עש״ה.

הרי שמתחכמים האלו לומר שמסיבת שפלותנו ואפסותנו אין מתאים לו ית׳ להשגיח עלינו ועזב אותנו, הם אינם אלא מכריזים על חוסר דעתם בלבד. ודמה לך אם היית פוגש איזה אדם שימציא לו לברוא בריות מלכתחילה בכדי שתתענינה ותתייסרנה בכל ימי חייהם, כמונו, ולא עוד אלא להשליך אותן אחר גיוו מבלי שירצה אפילו להשגיח בהן כדי לעזרן מעט – כמה היית מגנה ומזלזל בו. והיתכן להעלות על הדעת כזה על מחויב המציאות ית׳ וית׳.

ה׳

ולפיכך השכל הבריא מחייב אותנו להבין את ההיפך מהנראה בשטחיות, ולהחליט שאנו באמת בריות טובות ונעלות ביותר עד שאין קץ לחשיבותנו, דהיינו ממש באופן הראוי והמתאים לבעל המלאכה שעשה אותנו. כי כל משהו חסרון שתרצה להרהר על גופותנו, הנה אחר כל מיני תירוצים שאתה מתרץ לך, הוא נופל רק על הבורא ית׳ שברא אותנו ואת כל הטבעים שבנו. שהרי ברור

defective product will never emerge from a perfect builder. Every product attests to the nature of its maker. It is not the fault of a ratty item of clothing that it was prepared by an unqualified tailor. The Talmud makes this point (Taanit 20a):

> An incident occurred in which Rabbi Elazar, son of Rabbi Shimon… happened upon an exceedingly ugly person, who said to him, "Greetings to you, my rabbi," but Rabbi Elazar did not return his greeting. Instead, Rabbi Elazar said to him, "Worthless [*reika*] person, how ugly is that man. Are all the people of your city as ugly as you?" The man said to him, "I do not know, but you should go and say to the Craftsman Who made me: 'How ugly is the vessel you made!'" When Rabbi Elazar realized that he had sinned and insulted this man merely on account of his appearance, he descended from his donkey and prostrated himself before him, and he said to the man: "I have sinned against you; forgive me."

These "thinkers" claim that it is inappropriate for God to have providence over us and that He has abandoned us due to our lowliness and nothingness. This indicates only their own lack of understanding. Imagine meeting a person who suggests creating beings who are destined to suffer and experience pain for all of their lives, much as we do. Moreover, that person plans to forsake them, with no intention of offering his providence over them or assisting them in any way. We would certainly condemn and scorn such a person. Can we imagine saying such a thing about the necessary, existent God?!

5

Therefore, a clear-thinking individual must realize that the truth is the opposite of what appears on the surface. He must conclude that we are good and that we are the loftiest of creatures. We are of infinite significance. We are worthy of the Craftsman who made us. Any flaws in our bodies – whatever explanations we might offer for them – ultimately stem from the Creator who created us with all of our human nature. After

ש'הוא עשנו ולא אנחנו', גם ידע כל אלו התהלוכות אשר תמשכנה לצאת מכל אלו הטבעים והנטיות הרעות שנטע בנו.

אלא הוא הדבר אשר אמרנו, שצריכים אנו להסתכל על סוף המעשה ואז נוכל להבין הכל. ומשל בפי העולם: אל תראה דבר לשוטה באמצע מלאכתו.

ו'

וכבר הורונו חז"ל (עי' ע"ח שער הכללים פ"א בתחילתו), שלא ברא הקב"ה את העולם אלא בכדי לְהַנּוֹת לנבראיו. וכאן אנו צריכים להשים את עינינו וכל מחשבותינו, כי הוא סוף הכוונה והמעשה של בריאת העולם. ויש להתבונן, כיון שמחשבת הבריאה היתה בכדי להנות לנבראיו, הרי הכרח הוא שברא בנשמות מידת רצון גדולה עד מאד לקבל את אשר חשב ליתן להן. שהרי מידת גדלו של כל תענוג וכל הנאה מדודה במידת גדלו של הרצון לקבל אותו. עד שכל שהרצון לקבלו גדול יותר, הנה בשיעור הזה מידת התענוג גדולה ביותר, וכל שהרצון לקבלו פחות יותר, הרי באותה המידה נפחת שיעור התענוג מהקבלה. הרי שמחשבת הבריאה בעצמה מחייבת בהכרח לברוא בנשמות רצון לקבל בשיעור מופרז ביותר, המתאים למידת התענוג הגדול שכל יכלתו חשב לענג את הנשמות. כי התענוג הגדול והרצון לקבל הגדול עולים בקנה אחד.

הבריאה המחודשת

ז'

ואחר שידענו זה, כבר הגענו להבין חקירה הב' עד סופה בבירור מוחלט. כי חקרנו לדעת מה היא המציאות שאפשר להחליט עליה בבירור שאינה מצויה ואינה נכללת בעצמותו ית', עד שנאמר שהיא בריאה מחודשת יש מאין.

ועתה שידענו בבירור שמחשבת הבריאה שהיא בכדי להנות לנבראיו, בראה בהכרח מידת 'רצון לקבל' ממנו ית' את כל הנועם והטוב הזה שחשב

all, it is clear that "He made us, and we did not" (Ps. 100:3). He knows all of the consequences of our human nature and our bad tendencies, which He created within us.

Thus, what we stated before must be true: We must look at the purpose and end of creation in order to understand everything. As the saying goes: "Do not show anything to a fool while it is in the middle of being constructed."

6

The Sages (see [R. Ḥaim Vital's] *Etz Ḥayyim, Shaar HaKellalim* at the beginning of the first chapter) already explained that God created the world only in order to benefit His creatures. We must pay attention and focus on this, for it is the end and purpose of the creation of the world. [People] must understand that since the purpose of creation is to benefit creatures, it must be that [God] created in our souls a great desire to receive that which He intended to provide to them. After all, the greater the desire to receive a benefit, the greater the pleasure one derives from that benefit. One who has a greater desire to receive will have a proportionally greater pleasure from it, and one who has a lesser desire to receive will have a proportionally lesser pleasure from it. Hence, the intention behind creation requires creating souls with an enormous and exaggerated desire [for that pleasure], for that accords with the great pleasure with which the Almighty intended to pleasure the souls. Pleasure and the desire to receive are proportionate to one another.

RENEWED CREATION

7

Given the above, we can answer the second inquiry properly and clearly. We wanted to identify that reality about which it can be said that it does not exist and is not contained in God's essence, such that we can say that it was created "something from nothing," *ex nihilo*.

Now that we know that the intention behind creation was to give pleasure to His creatures, He must have created a "desire to receive" from God all of the pleasure and good that He intended for them. This

בעדם. הנה הרצון לקבל הזה, ודאי שלא היה כלול בעצמותו ית׳ מטרם שבראו בנשמות, כי ממי יקבל? הרי שברא דבר מחודש שאינו בו ית׳.

ויחד עם זה מובן על פי מחשבת הבריאה, שלא היה צריך כלל לברוא משהו יותר מהרצון לקבל הזה. שהרי בריאה מחודשת הזו, כבר מספקת לו ית׳ למלאות כל מחשבת הבריאה שחשב עלינו להנות אותנו. אבל כל המילוי שבמחשבת הבריאה, דהיינו כל מיני הטבות שחשב בעדנו, כבר הן נמשכות בהמשכה ישרה מעצמותו ית׳, ואין לו ענין לברוא אותן מחדש בעת שכבר הן נמשכות יש מיש אל הרצון לקבל הגדול שבנשמות. והנה נתברר לנו בהחלט, שכל החומר כולו, מתחילתו עד סופו, שבבריאה המחודשת – הוא רק ׳הרצון לקבל׳.

הנשמות – חלק אלקי ממעל

ח׳

ומכאן באנו גם לסוף דעתם של המקובלים שהבאנו בחקירה הג׳. שתמהנו עליהם, איך אפשר לומר על הנשמות שהן חלק אלקי ממעל, בהשוואה אל האבן שנחצבה מההר שאין הפרש ביניהם אלא שזה ׳חלק׳ וזה ׳כל׳. ותמהנו, תינח האבן שנפרדה מההר, שנעשית חלק ממנו על ידי גרזן מוכן לכך, אבל בעצמותו ית׳ איך יתכן לומר כך, ובמה נחלקו הנשמות מעצמותו ית׳ ויצאו מכלל בורא ית׳ להיות נבראים.

ובהמתבאר מובן הדבר היטב. כי כמו שהגרזן מחתך ומבדיל בדבר גשמי לחלקו לשנים, כן שינוי הצורה מבדיל ברוחני לחלקו לשנים. למשל, כשב׳ אנשים אוהבים זה את זה, תאמר שהם דבקים זה בזה כגוף אחד. ולהיפך כשהם שונאים זה את זה, תאמר שהם רחוקים איש מרעהו כרחוק מזרח ממערב. ואין כאן ענין של קרבת מקום או ריחוק מקום, אלא הכוונה היא על השתוות הצורה: שבהיותם שווים בצורתם איש לרעהו, שאוהב כל מה שחברו אוהב ושונא כל

desire to receive could not have been contained in God's essence prior to the creation of [human] souls, for from whom could He have received [given that there was nothing other than God]? He then created something new that had not been part of Him.

Given this, there was no need to create anything other than that desire to receive in order to achieve the goal of creation. This new creation [of a desire to receive] itself supplied to God all that was needed to fulfill the goal of creation, which He had planned in order to benefit us. All of the content of the plan of creation – that is, all of the good He intended for us – would flow directly from God's essence, and He would not have to create them anew, since they would flow from pre-existing reality to the great desire to receive [that is already in] souls. It follows absolutely that all of material existence, from beginning to end, in this unique creation is [really] nothing other than "the desire to receive."

THE SOULS – PART OF GOD ABOVE

8

This explains the position of the kabbalists discussed in inquiry number three. We asked: How can we speak of the souls as part of God above? We compared this to a stone quarried from a mountain, regarding which there is no distinction between them. Instead, this [the stones] are "part" of that "whole" [the mountain]. We then asked: When the stone separates from the mountain, it is separated only due to acts that are designed to separate it. But we cannot say such a thing about God's essence! How did the souls separate from the essence of God, becoming creatures distinct from the Creator?

We can now understand this precisely. Just as an axe splits and divides a physical object into two parts, a change in form [essence] separates a spiritual thing into two. For example, when two people love one another, one can say that they are connected to each another as one body. When they hate each another, one can say that they are as distant from each other as west is from east. This is not a description of their physical closeness or distance, but a similarity in their forms. Since the two of them are similar in form to one another – each loves

מה שחברו שונא וכדומה - נמצאים אוהבים זה את זה ודבוקים זה בזה. ואם יש ביניהם איזה שינוי צורה, דהיינו שאוהב דבר־מה אע״פ שחברו שונא הדבר וכדומה, הרי בשיעור שינוי הצורה הזה הם שנואים ורחוקים זה מזה. ואם למשל הם בהפכיות הצורה, דהיינו כל מה שזה אוהב נמצא שנוא לחברו, וכל מה שזה שונא נמצא אהוב לחברו - הרי אז רחוקים זה מזה כרחוק מזרח ממערב, דהיינו מקצה אל הקצה.

ט׳

והנך מוצא שברוחניות פועל שינוי הצורה כמו הגרזן המפריד בין הגשמיים, וכן שיעור ההרחקה הוא כפי שיעור הפכיות הצורה. ומכאן תשכיל, כיון שנטבע בנשמות הרצון לקבל הנאתו כנ״ל, אשר הוכחנו בעליל שצורה זו אינה נמצאת כלל בהבורא ית׳, כי ח״ו ממי יקבל - הרי שינוי צורה הזה שהשיגו הנשמות, פועל להפרידם מעצמותו ית׳ כדמיון הגרזן החוצב האבן מן ההר. באופן שע״י שינוי הצורה הזה יצאו הנשמות מכלל בורא ונבדלו הימנו להיות נבראים. אמנם כל מה שמשיגות הנשמות מאורו ית׳, הרי הוא נמשך יש מיש מעצמותו ית׳.

אם כן נמצא, שמבחינת אורו ית׳ שמקבלות תוך הכלי שבהן, שהוא הרצון לקבל, אין הפרש כלל ביניהן לעצמותו ית׳, שהרי הוא מקובל להן יש מיש ישר מעצמותו ית׳. וכל ההפרש שבין הנשמות לעצמותו ית׳ אינו יותר אלא במה שהנשמות הן חלק מעצמותו ית׳, דהיינו ששיעור האור שקבלו תוך הכלי שהוא הרצון לקבל כבר הוא חלק נבדל מאלקי, בהיותו נשוא תוך שינוי הצורה של הרצון לקבל, ששינוי צורה זה עשה אותו לחלק, שעל ידו יצאו מבחי׳ ׳כל׳ ונעשו לבחינת ׳חלק׳. הרי שאין ביניהם אלא שזה ׳כל׳ וזה ׳חלק׳, כאבן הנחצבת מההר. והתבונן היטב, כי אי אפשר להאריך יותר במקום גבוה כזה.

what the other one loves and hates what the other one hates, etc. – they love one another and cleave to one another. If their form changes, such that one loves what the other hates or the like, they will become proportionally distant from one another, to the point of hatred. If they are opposites in form – such that whatever one likes, the other hates, and vice versa – then they are extremely distant from one another, as far as east is from west.

9

Differences in form act spiritually much as the axe acts physically to separate things. The distance [between the two spiritual things] will be proportional to the difference in form. Understand, as discussed, that souls are imbued with a desire to receive pleasure, which, as we demonstrated, does not exist at all within the Creator. Heaven forfend! From whom could God receive?! This change in form that the souls acquire serves to separate them from God's essence, much as the axe separates a stone from the mountain. This change in form detaches the souls from God, and they become creatures separate from Him. Still, anything that the souls acquire from God's light flows from a pre-existing reality, from God's essence.

If so, it follows that from the perspective of the divine light received by the vessel – which is the desire to receive – there is absolutely no difference between the soul and God's essence, as it [the divine light] flows from the pre-existing reality of God's essence directly to the souls. The entire difference between the soul and God's essence is that the soul is only a part of God's essence. The limited amount of divine light received by the vessel, the desire to receive, becomes a separate entity from the Divine due to this change of form. Through it [this change in form], the light transformed from being in the category of "All" to being in the category of "part." Thus, the only difference between them is that one is "all" and the other is "part," like a stone that is quarried from the mountain. Study this carefully, since I cannot expound more about such lofty things.

טעם התהוות מערכת הטומאה והקליפות

י׳

ועתה נפתח לנו הפתח להבין החקירה הד׳. איך אפשר שיתהווה מקדושתו ית׳ ענין מרכבת הטומאה והקליפות, אחר שהיא רחוקה מקדושתו ית׳ מקצה אל הקצה. ואיך יתכן שיפרנס אותה ויקיימה.

אכן יש להבין מקודם ענין מציאות מהות הטומאה והקליפות מה היא. ותדע שהרצון לקבל הגדול הזה, שאמרנו שהוא עצם מהותן של הנשמות מבחינת עצם בריאתן, כי על כן הן מוכנות לקבל כל המילוי שבמחשבת הבריאה – הוא לא נשאר בצורתו זו בנשמות. כי אם היה נשאר בהן, היו מוכרחות להישאר תמיד בפרודא (פירוד) ממנו ית׳, כי שינוי הצורה שבהן היה מפרידן ממנו ית׳.

ובכדי לתקן דבר הפירוד הזה המונח על הכלי של הנשמות, ברא ית׳ את כל העולמות כולם והבדילם לב׳ מערכות. בסוד הכתוב (קהלת ז, יד): ״זה לעומת זה עשה אלהים״. שהן ד׳ עולמות אבי״ע (אצילות בריאה יצירה עשיה) דקדושה, ולעומתן ד׳ עולמות אבי״ע דטומאה. והטביע את הרצון להשפיע במערכת אבי״ע דקדושה, והסיר מהם את הרצון לקבל לעצמו (כמ״ש בפתיחה לחכמת הקבלה אותיות יד-יט עש״ה) ונתן אותו במערכת העולמות אבי״ע דטומאה, ונמצאו בגללו נפרדים מהבורא ית׳ ומכל העולמות דקדושה.

ומטעם זה מכונות הקליפות בשם מתים, כמ״ש ״זבחי מתים״. וכן הרשעים הנמשכים אחריהם, כמ״ש חז״ל (ברכות יח, ב): ״הרשעים בחייהם נקראים מתים״. כי הרצון לקבל המוטבע בהם [שהוא] בהפכיות הצורה מקדושתו ית׳, מפרידן מחיי החיים והן רחוקות ממנו ית׳ מקצה אל הקצה. כי הוא ית׳ אין לו שום ענין של קבלה אלא רק להשפיע לבד, והקליפות אין להן שום ענין של השפעה רק לקבל לעצמן להנאתן בלבד, ואין הפכיות גדולה מזו. וכבר ידעת שהמרחק הרוחני מתחיל בשינוי צורה במשהו, ומסתיים בהפכיות הצורה שהיא סוף המרחק בדיוטא האחרונה.

THE REASON THE SYSTEM OF IMPURITY AND THE "HUSKS" COME INTO BEING

10

We are now in a position to answer query four. How can the system [lit. chariot] of impurity and the husks emerge from the sanctity of God, since they are so radically distant from God's sanctity? How can God maintain and nourish them?

We must first understand the true essence of impurity and husks. Know that the desire to receive – which, as we said, is the essence of the souls as they were created, since that enables them to receive all of the fullness planned for creation – does not remain as it was [originally] in the souls. Had it [the desire to receive] remained the same, they [the souls] would always remain separate from God, since their change in form separates them from God.

In order to repair the separation [from God] that is present in the vessel of the souls, God created all of the worlds and divided them into two systems, as the verse states: "God made both, one opposite the other" (Eccl. 7:14). These are the four holy worlds of *ABYA* (*Atzilut* [Emanation], *Beria* [Creation], *Yetzira* [Formation], and *Asiya* [Action]), as well as their counterparts – four impure *ABYA* worlds. God established a desire to give in the holy system of *ABYA*, and He removed from them a selfish desire to receive (as I will explain in chapters 14–19 below). He placed that [desire to receive] in the impure *ABYA* worlds, which separated them from God and from the worlds of sanctity.

This is why the husks are referred to as "dead," as the verse describes: "sacrifices of the dead" (Ps. 106:28). Similarly, evildoers are attracted to them [the husks], as the Sages state: "The wicked, [even] during their lives, are called dead" (Berakhot 18b). This is because their inherent desire to receive, which is the opposite of the form that stems from God's sanctity, separates them from the Life-Force of the Living; they exist at opposite poles from God. For God has no desire to receive, but only to give to others. And the husks contain no element of giving, but only receiving for their own pleasure. These are extreme opposites. It is known that spiritual distance starts with a small difference in form and ends with a form that is radically opposite, at an extreme distance, on another level entirely.

י"א

ונשתלשלו העולמות עד למציאות עולם הזה הגשמי, דהיינו למקום שתהיה בו מציאות גוף ונשמה, וכן זמן קלקול ותיקון. כי הגוף, שהוא הרצון לקבל לעצמו, נמשך משורשו שבמחשבת הבריאה כנ"ל, ועובר דרך המערכה של העולמות דטומאה, כמ"ש (איוב יא, יב): "עַיִר פֶּרֶא אָדָם יִוָּלֵד", ונשאר משועבד תחת המערכה ההיא עד י"ג שנה. והוא זמן הקלקול.

ועל ידי עסק המצוות מי"ג שנים ואילך, שעוסק על מנת להשפיע נחת רוח ליוצרו, הוא מתחיל לטהר הרצון לקבל לעצמו המוטבע בו ומהפכו לאט לאט על מנת להשפיע. שבזה הולך וממשיך נפש קדושה משורשה במחשבת הבריאה, והיא עוברת דרך המערכה של העולמות דקדושה והיא מתלבשת בגוף. והוא הזמן של התיקון.

וכן מוסיף והולך לקנות ולהשיג מדרגות דקדושה ממחשבת הבריאה שבא"ס ב"ה (אין סוף ברוך הוא), עד שהן מסייעות לו להאדם להפוך את הרצון לקבל לעצמו שבו, שיהיה כולו בבחינת מקבל על מנת להשפיע נחת רוח ליוצרו ולא כלל לתועלת עצמו. שבזה קונה האדם השוואת הצורה ליוצרו. כי קבלה על מנת להשפיע נחשבת לצורת השפעה טהורה (כמ"ש במסכת קדושין (דף ז, א) שבאדם חשוב, נתנה היא ואמר הוא, הרי זו מקודשת. כי קבלתו שהיא על מנת לְהַנּוֹת לנותנת לו, נחשבת להשפעה ונתינה גמורה אליה, עש"ה), ואז קונה דבקות גמורה בו ית'. כי דבקות הרוחני אינה אלא השוואת הצורה (כמ"ש חז"ל (ע"פ סוטה יד, א): "ואיך אפשר להדבק בו? אלא הדבק במידותיו", ע"ש). שבזה נעשה האדם ראוי לקבל כל הטוב והנועם והרוך שבמחשבת הבריאה.

11

The worlds developed [*nishtalshelu*] until this material world came into being, a place that contains both body and soul, and a time wherein both corruption and repair are possible. The body, which is the desire to receive, derived from its roots in God's plan for creation, as discussed earlier. But it [the body] passed through the worlds of impurity, as Job states: "A wild ass gives birth to a human" (Job 11:12). [The words "wild ass" refer to the worlds of impurity.] It [the body] remains enslaved under that system until age thirteen. That is the period of corruption.

After age thirteen, a person's performance of mitzvot – performed with the intention to give satisfaction to his Maker – begins purifying the selfish desire to receive that had been imprinted in him. [Performance of mitzvot] gradually turns [that selfish desire] into a desire to give. This gradually draws [*mamshikh*] the holy soul from its roots in the plan of creation. It [the holy soul] traverses the entire system of sanctified worlds and becomes enclothed in the body. That is the time of repair.

From then on, he continually acquires and reaches levels of sanctity that are part of the plan of creation and are present in the *Ein Sof* [the Infinite]. These [levels of sanctity] assist the person in transforming the selfish desire to receive that is embedded in him into a desire to give, to the point that he becomes one who receives only in order to give satisfaction to his Maker rather than to benefit himself. In this way, a person equates his own form to [that of] his Maker. For receiving for the sake of giving to others is considered the purest form of giving. (This is related to what is stated in Kiddushin 7a: If a woman gives a gift to an important man, she receives benefit from the fact that he consents to accept a gift from her. That benefit is adequate to be considered the exchange that is legally required for them to be married. The fact that he accepts the gift in order for her to benefit from the fact that she gave it to him is considered a complete gift to her.) The person then achieves a complete bond with God. For a spiritual bond is nothing other than an equating of form. To paraphrase a statement of the Sages: "How can one cleave to God? Rather, cleave to His attributes" (based on Sota 14a). That is how a person can become worthy to receive all of the good, pleasantness, and softness that was in the plan of creation.

י״ב

והנה נתבאר היטב דבר התיקון של הרצון לקבל המוטבע בנשמות מצד מחשבת הבריאה. כי הכין הבורא ית׳ בשבילן ב׳ מערכות הנ״ל, זה לעומת זה, שעל ידיהן עוברות הנשמות ומתחלקות לב׳ בחינות, גוף ונפש, המתלבשים זה בזה. וע״י תורה ומצוות נמצאים בסופם שיהפכו צורת הרצון לקבל כמו צורת הרצון להשפיע. אז יכולים לקבל כל הטוב שבמחשבת הבריאה – ויחד עם זה זוכים לדבקות חזקה בו ית׳, מפאת שזכו ע״י העבודה בתורה ומצוות להשוואת הצורה ליוצרם. שזה נבחן לגמר התיקון. ואז כיון שלא יהיה עוד שום צורך לסטרא אחרא הטמאה, היא תתבער מן הארץ ויבולע המוות לנצח. וכל העבודה בתורה ומצוות שניתנה לכלל העולם במשך שִׁיתָּא אַלְפֵי שְׁנֵי דְּהָוֵי עָלְמָא (ששת אלפים שנה שהעולם קיים), וכן לכל פרט במשך שבעים שנות חייו – אינה אלא להביאם לגמר התיקון של השוואת הצורה האמורה.

גם נתבאר היטב, ענין התהוות ויציאת מערכת הקליפות והטומאה מקדושתו ית׳. שהיה מוכרח זה כדי להמשיך על ידה בריאת הגופים, שאח״כ יתקנו אותו [את הרצון לקבל] ע״י תורה ומצוות. ואם לא היו נמשכים לנו הגופים ברצון לקבל שבהם המקולקל ע״י מערכת הטומאה, אז לא היה אפשר לנו לתקנו לעולם. כי אין אדם מתקן מה שאין בו.

12

We now understand that the desire to receive, which is embedded in the soul due to the plan of creation, requires repair. For God has created the two systems [the system of purity and the system of impurity, the *sitra aḥra*], one opposite the other, through which the souls pass. Through them, they are separated into two aspects, the body and the soul, which become intertwined [*mitlabshot,* lit. enclothed in one another]. Through Torah and mitzvot, the desire to receive is eventually transformed into a desire to give. Then [after that transformation], the souls can receive all of the good that is in the plan of creation, and they also become worthy of a stronger bond with God, since the service of Torah and mitzvot transform the form [of the soul] into that of the Creator. This is the last stage of repair. Then there will be no need for the impure "Other Side," which will be eliminated from the earth, and death shall be swallowed up forever. All of the service of Torah and mitzvot – which was granted to the entire world during the six thousand years of the world's existence, and to each individual for the seventy years of his life – is for the purpose of bringing about that final stage of repair, in which people's forms become equated [with that of God], as discussed.

This also explains how the system of husks and impurity emanate from God's sanctity. They are a necessary precursor to the creation of bodies, which can then be repaired (along with the desire to receive) through Torah and mitzvot. If bodies with a defective desire to receive had not emanated from the system of impurity, we would be unable to repair them, since a person cannot repair what he does not possess.

פרק ב'

הרצון לקבל המתוקן

י"ג

אמנם עדיין נשאר לנו להבין: סוף סוף, כיון שהרצון לקבל לעצמו הוא כל כך פגום ומקולקל, איך יצא והיה במחשבת הבריאה בא"ס ב"ה, שלאחדותו אין הגה ומילה לפרשה.

והענין הוא, כי באמת תכף בהמחשבה לברוא את הנשמות, היתה מחשבתו ית' גומרת הכל. כי אינו צריך לכלי מעשה כמונו. ותיכף יצאו ונתהוו כל הנשמות וכל העולמות העתידים להבראות, מלאים בכל הטוב והעונג והרוך שחשב בעדן, עם כל תכלית שלמותן הסופית שהנשמות עתידות לקבל בגמר התיקון, דהיינו אחר שהרצון לקבל שבנשמות כבר קיבל כל תיקונו בשלמות ונתהפך להיות השפעה טהורה, בהשוואת הצורה הגמורה אל המאציל ית'

Part 2

The Repaired Desire to Receive

Human perfection and the perfection of creation result from repairing the inborn desire to receive, transforming it into a desire to give to others. This process occurs gradually, through a step-by-step improvement of the human body and character, concluding with the messianic resurrection of the dead in a purified state.

13

We must still understand: If the selfish desire to receive is itself so negative and defective, how did the *Ein Sof* conceive of it in the plan of creation? The *Ein Sof* is absolutely unified, in ways that humans cannot describe!

The explanation is as follows: Prior to [God's] thought to create the souls, His thought encompassed everything, for He needs no tools like we do. [As soon as He thought,] immediately, all of the souls emerged and came into being, as did all of the future worlds that would be created, filled with all of the good, pleasure, and tenderness that He had planned for them [the souls]. [These worlds would] contain the endpoint of the souls' perfection, which the souls would receive at the end of the repair. [The end of the repair would occur] after the desire to receive would already be completely and perfectly repaired and transformed into a pure desire to give; [at that point,] the form [of the souls] would become identical to that of God, from which all emanates

(זוהר משפטים אות נא; ז"ח בראשית אות רמג). והוא מטעם כי בנצחיותו ית' העבר והעתיד וההווה משמשים כאחד, והעתיד משמש לו כהווה, ואין ענין 'מחוסר זמן' נוהג בו ית'. ומטעם זה לא היה כלל ענין הרצון לקבל המקולקל בצורה דפרודא בא"ס ב"ה, אלא להיפך, שאותה השוואת הצורה העתידה להגלות בגמר התיקון הופיעה תיכף בנצחיותו ית'. ועל סוד הזה אמרו חז"ל (בפרקי דר' אליעזר פ"ג): "קודם שנברא העולם היה הוא ושמו אחד". כי הצורה דְּפֵירוּדָא שברצון לקבל לא נתגלתה כלל במציאות הנשמות שיצאו במחשבת הבריאה, אלא הן היו דבוקות בו בהשוואת הצורה, בסוד "הוא ושמו אחד". עי' בתלמוד עשר הספירות חלק א' (הסת"פ אות יג).

ג' מצבי הנשמות

י"ד

והנך מוצא בהכרח שיש ג' מצבים לנשמות בדרך כלל. מצב הא' הוא: מציאותן בא"ס ב"ה במחשבת הבריאה. שכבר יש להן שם צורה העתידה של גמר התיקון.

מצב הב' הוא: מציאותן בבחינת שִׁיתָּא אַלְפֵי שְׁנֵי. שנתחלקו ע"י ב' המערכות הנ"ל לגוף ונפש, וניתנה להן העבודה בתורה ומצוות כדי להפך את הרצון לקבל שבהן, ולהביאו לבחינת רצון להשפיע נחת רוח ליוצרן ולא לעצמן כלל. ובמשך זמן מצב הזה לא יגיע שום תיקון לגופים, רק לנפשות בלבד. כלומר שצריכות לבער מקרבן כל בחינת הקבלה לעצמן, שהיא בחינת הגוף, ולהישאר בבחינת רצון אך להשפיע בלבד שזוהי צורת הרצון שבנפשות. ואפילו נפשות הצדיקים לא תוכלנה להתענג בגן עדן אחר פטירתן אלא אחר ככלות כל גופן להירקב בעפר.

(Zohar, *Mishpatim*, 51; Zohar Ḥadash, *Bereishit*, 243). This is because the divine eternality contains past, present, and future as one. The future is, for Him, like the present, and "time for things to develop" is inapplicable to God.

For this reason, the defective desire to receive in its differentiated form [*tzura d'peruda*] was never present in the *Ein Sof*. On the contrary, the equation of the forms that will be revealed in the future, at the end of the repair, was immediately present in God's eternality. The Sages explained this esoteric idea in *Pirkei DeRabbi Eliezer* 73. "Prior to creation, He was one and His name was one." The differentiated form of the desire to receive was not revealed at all in the reality of the souls as they emerged from the plan of creation. Rather, they clung to God through the equation of forms, which is the secret of "He and His name are one." See my *Talmud Eser HaSefirot*, Part 1.

THE THREE STATES OF THE SOULS

14

It necessarily follows that souls can generally exist in three states:

1. Their existence within the Infinite as part of the plan of creation. They already have their future form, [the one that they will have] after the repair is complete.
2. Their existence during the six thousand years [of this world's existence], in which they are separated into the two systems, yielding the body and the soul. In that state, they are given the service of Torah and mitzvot so that they can transform their [selfish] desire to receive into a[n altruistic] desire to give satisfaction to their Creator and not for themselves at all. During this time, their bodies will not be repaired at all; only the souls will. That is to say, [the souls] must eliminate from themselves any element of selfish receiving, which is the aspect of the body, and remain with only an element of giving, which is the form of the souls' desire. Even the souls of the righteous cannot enjoy the pleasures of Eden after death until their bodies have completely decomposed in the grave.

מצב הג׳ הוא: גמר התיקון של הנשמות אחר תחיית המתים. שאז יגיע התיקון השלם גם אל הגופים. כי אז יהפכו גם את הקבלה עצמה, שהיא צורת הגוף, שתשרה עליה צורה של השפעה טהורה. ונעשים ראויים לקבל לעצמם כל הטוב והעונג והנועם שבמחשבת הבריאה – ועם כל זה יזכו לדבקות החזקה, מכוח השוואת צורתם ליוצרם. כי לא יקבלו כל זה מצד רצונם לקבל, אלא מצד רצונם להשפיע נחת רוח ליוצרם. שהרי יש לו ית׳ הנאה שמקבלים ממנו.

ולשם הקיצור אשתמש מכאן ואילך בשמות ג׳ המצבים הללו, דהיינו: מצב א׳, מצב ב׳ ומצב ג׳. ואתה תזכור כל המתבאר כאן בכל מצב ומצב.

ט״ו

וכשתסתכל בג׳ מצבים הללו, תמצא שמחייבים זה את זה בהחלט גמור. באופן שאם היה אפשר שיתבטל משהו מאחד מהם, היו מתבטלים כולם. כי למשל, אם לא היה מתגלה מצב הג׳ שהוא התהפכות צורת הקבלה לצורת השפעה, הרי בהכרח לא היה יכול לצאת מצב הא׳ שבא״ס ב״ה. שהרי לא יצאה שם כל השלמות אלא מפני שהעתיד להיות במצב הג׳ כבר שימש שם בנצחיותו ית׳ כמו הווה, וכל השלמות שנצטיירה שם באותו המצב היא רק כמו העתקה מהעתיד לבוא אל ההווה אשר שם – אבל באם היה אפשר שיתבטל העתיד, לא היתה שם שום מציאות בהווה. הרי שמצב הג׳ מחייב כל המציאות שבמצב הא׳. ומכל־שכן בהתבטל משהו ממצב הב׳, ששם מציאות כל העבודה העתידה להגמר במצב הג׳, דהיינו העבודה בקלקול ותיקון ובהמשכות מדרגות הנשמות – איך יהיה מצב הג׳? הרי שמצב הב׳ מחייב את מצב הג׳.

3. Complete repair of the souls following the resurrection of the dead. Then, even the bodies shall be repaired, and even the receiving itself, which is the form of the body, will be transformed such that a form of pure giving will rest upon it [the body]. The souls will then become worthy of receiving for themselves all of the good, pleasure, and pleasantness that is in the plan of creation, while still being worthy of this strong bond [with God], since they will be identical in form to their Creator. For they will not receive all this [pleasure that is in the plan of creation] out of their own desire to receive, but out of their desire to give pleasure to their Creator. After all, God has pleasure when others receive from Him.

To simplify the discussion, from now on, I will use the terms "first state," "second state," and "third state." Later, recall how I have defined these terms here.

15

When one examines these three states, he will realize that they are dependent on one another. If one of them were absent, the others would of necessity also be absent. For example, without the third state, in which the form of receiving is transformed into the form of giving, the first state could never have emerged from the *Ein Sof* [Infinite]. All of the various perfections only emerged [from the *Ein Sof*] because they would eventually reach the third state. Within the eternality of God, the future [third state] was already there in the present. The perfection perceived in that [first] form was simply "copied" [*haataka*] from the future [third state] into the present that was there [in the first state]. If it were conceivable that the future would not happen, then there would be no existence [of the perfected souls] in the present [first state]. That is, the third state requires the reality of the first state. How much more so regarding the hypothetical elimination of something from the second state, which contains all of the service [of God] that is meant to lead to the third stage – the process of defects and gradual repair of the souls from level to level. [If the second state would not exist,] how could the third state occur? Hence, the second state requires the third to occur.

וכן מציאות מצב הא׳ שבא״ס ב״ה שכבר נוהגת שם כל השלמות שבמצב הג׳, הרי היא מחייבת בהחלט שיותאם זה, דהיינו שיתגלו מצב הב׳ ומצב הג׳. דהיינו ממש בכל אותה השלמות אשר שם, לא פחות משהו ולא יותר משהו. הרי שמצב הא׳ עצמו מחייב בהכרח שתתפשטנה מערכות זו לעומת זו במציאות הב׳, כדי לאפשר מציאות גוף ברצון לקבל המקולקל ע״י מערכת הטומאה, ואז אפשר לנו לתקנו. ואם לא היתה מערכת העולמות דטומאה, לא היה לנו הרצון לקבל הזה, ולא היה אפשר לתקנו ולבוא למצב הג׳. כי אין אדם מתקן מה שאין בו. הרי שאין לשאול איך נתהותה ממצב הא׳ מערכת הטומאה, כי אדרבה מצב הא׳ הוא המחייב מציאותה ולהתקיים כן במצב הב׳.

הבחירה

ט״ז

ואין להקשות לפי זה, אם כן נתבטלה מאתנו הבחירה ח״ו, כיון שאנו מוכרחים להשתלם ולקבל המצב הג׳ בהחלט, מכוח שכבר הוא מצוי במצב הא׳. והענין הוא, כי ב׳ דרכים הכין לנו השי״ת במצב הב׳ כדי להביאנו אל מצב הג׳: הא׳ היא דרך קיום התורה ומצוות, על דרך שנתבאר לעיל. ודרך הב׳ היא דרך יסורין. אשר היסורים בעצמם ממרקין את הגוף, ויכריחו אותנו לבסוף להפך את הרצון לקבל שבנו ולקבל צורת הרצון להשפיע, ולהדבק בו ית׳. והוא על דרך שאמרו חז״ל (סנהדרין צז, ב): אם אתם חוזרים למוטב, טוב, ואם לאו אני מעמיד עליכם מלך כהמן ובעל כרחכם הוא יחזיר אתכם למוטב.

וזה שאמרו ז״ל (שם צח, א) על הכתוב: ״בְּעִתָּהּ אֲחִישֶׁנָּה״ – אם זכו ׳אחישנה׳, ואם לאו ׳בעתה׳. פירוש, אם זוכים על ידי דרך הא׳, שהוא ע״י קיום תורה ומצוות, אז אנו ממהרים את התיקון שלנו, ואין אנו צריכים ליסורין קשים ומרים ואריכות הזמן שיספיק לקבלם, שיחזירו אותנו למוטב בעל כרחנו. ואם

In addition, if the first state in the *Ein Sof* already contains all of the perfections of the third state, it follows that the second and third states must occur, with all of the perfections that are already present there [in the first stage]. That is to say, the first state itself requires that the two competing systems [of the body and soul] must separate in the second stage, so that the body – which exists as a defective desire to receive, damaged by the system of impurity – could then be repaired. Were it not for the system of the worlds of impurity, we would never possess that desire to receive, and it would therefore be impossible to repair that desire and bring about the third stage, because a person cannot repair what he does not possess. Thus, do not ask how the system of impurity emerges out of the first stage, since the opposite is the case. The first stage requires the existence [of the system of impurity] in the second stage.

FREE WILL

16

Do not ask the following question: According to this, do we not (God forbid) have free will, since we are completely destined to become perfect and enter the third state, since it [the perfection of the third stage] is already present in the first stage?

The explanation is as follows: God prepared two paths in the second stage to bring us to the third stage. The first is through fulfilling Torah and mitzvot, as explained above. The second is through suffering. The suffering itself purifies the body, and it forces us to eventually transform our desire to receive into the form of the desire to give, and therefore to bond with God. This is related to what the Sages state (Sanhedrin 97b): "If the Jewish people repent, good [they will be redeemed]; if not, I will appoint a king over you like Haman [who will afflict you with harsh punishments] and force you to repent."

"In its time, I will hasten it" (Is. 60:22). The Sages explain (Sanhedrin 98a): "If they are worthy, I will hasten it [the redemption]; if they are not worthy, it will be at its time." This means that if we are worthy of using the first path, i.e., that of Torah and mitzvot, then we hasten our repair, and we will not require severe, bitter suffering over a long period of time

לאו - 'בעתה', דהיינו רק בעת שהיסורים יגמרו את התיקון שלנו ותגיע לנו עת התיקון בעל כרחנו. ובכלל דרך היסורים הם גם עונשי הנשמות בגיהנם. אבל בין כך ובין כך, גמר התיקון שהוא מצב הג' הוא מחויב ומוחלט מצד המצב הא', וכל הבחירה שלנו היא רק בין דרך יסורין לבין תורה ומצוות.

והנה נתבאר היטב איך ג' המצבים הללו של הנשמות קשורים זה בזה ומחייבים בהחלט זה את זה.

הגוף האמיתי

י"ז

ובהמתבאר מובנת היטב קושיא ג' הנ"ל, שהקשינו שבעת שאנו מסתכלים על עצמנו, אנו מוצאים את עצמנו מקולקלים ונבזים שאין כמונו לגנות. ובעת שאנו מסתכלים על הפועל שפעל אותנו, הרי אנו צריכים להיות ברום המעלות שאין כמונו לשבח, כיאות להפועל שברא אותנו. כי מטבע הפועל השלם שפעולותיו שלמות.

ובהאמור מובן היטב, שאותו הגוף שלנו בכל מקריו וקנייניו האפסיים אינו כלל הגוף שלנו האמיתי. שהרי הגוף שלנו האמיתי, כלומר הנצחי השלם בכל מיני שלמות, כבר הוא מצוי עומד וקיים בא"ס ב"ה בבחינת מצב הא', שמקבל שם צורתו השלמה מהעתיד להיות במצב הג', דהיינו קבלה בצורת השפעה, שהיא בהשוואת הצורה לא"ס ב"ה. ואם אמנם מצבנו הא' עצמו מחייב שתנתן לנו במציאות הב' את הקליפה של אותו הגוף שלנו, בצורתה הבזויה והמקולקלת שהוא הרצון לקבל אך לעצמו, שהוא כוח הפירוד מא"ס ב"ה כנ"ל, בכדי לתקנו ולאפשר לנו לקבל הגוף הנצחי שלנו בפועל גמור במצב הג' - אין לנו להתרעם על כך כלל. כי העבודה שלנו לא תצויר, רק בגוף הזה הכלה ונפסד, כי אין אדם מתקן מה שאין בו. באופן שבאמת אנו מצויים באותו שיעור השלמות הראוי ומתאים להפועל השלם שפעל אותנו גם במצבנו זה הב'. כי גוף זה אינו פוגם

to force us to return to the proper path. If not, however, [the repair] will occur at its time – that is, at the time that the suffering will bring about the repair, and the time of repair will arrive against our will. (That path of suffering includes the punishments of the souls in *gehinnom.*) In either case, the repair will be completed in the third stage, which is inevitable given the first stage, and our free will determines whether [the third stage] arrives through suffering or through Torah and mitzvot.

We thus explained how the three stages of the souls are interconnected and even necessarily follow from one another.

THE TRUE BODY

17

Given the above, we can now answer our third inquiry. We had asked: When we look at ourselves, we see ourselves as defective. There is little more despicable than we are. Yet, when we look at the Creator who created us, we expect ourselves [as His creatures] to be most lofty, worthy of the highest praise. After all, given our Creator, [we ought to be perfect,] since it is only natural for a perfect being to produce perfect products.

Based on the above, this is explained. Our body – with all of its contingencies and with the insignificant things it has acquired – is not our true body. Our true body – the eternal and wholly perfect one – is already present in the *Ein Sof* as part of the first stage. It receives its form there [in the *Ein Sof*], which is the form that it will take in the future in the third stage. [That form is] receiving in the form of giving [i.e., the good that one gains by giving to others], which is identical to the form of the *Ein Sof*. True, our situation in the first stage requires that in the second stage, we will receive the husk [*kelipa*] of that perfect body, with its despicable and defective form – the selfish desire to receive. That [desire] is the force that separates [the soul] from the *Ein Sof*. That then leads to the repair of the body, which enables us to receive the eternal, completely actualized body in the third stage. Therefore, we should not complain about this at all. For our service [of God] is unimaginable without this disposable and faulty body, since a person cannot repair what he does not contain. That is to say, even our body in the second stage is in fact perfect, as befitting the perfect Creator who made us. This [physical]

אותנו במשהו, שהרי הוא עומד למות ולהתבטל, ואינו מוכן לנו רק בשיעור זמן הנחוץ לבטלו ולקבל צורתנו הנצחית.

בריות נצחיות

י"ח

ויחד עם זה מיושבת קושיא ה', שהקשינו איך אפשר שמנצחי תצאנה פעולות בלתי נצחיות, הוות ונפסדות. ובהמתבאר מובן, כי באמת כבר יצאנו מלפניו כראוי לנצחיותו, דהיינו בריות נצחיות בכל השלמות. ונצחיותנו זו מחייבת בהכרח שקליפת הגוף שניתנה לנו רק לעבודה, תהיה כלה ונפסדת. כי אם היתה נשארת בנצחיות ח"ו אז היינו נשארים נפרדים ח"ו מחי החיים לנצחיות. וכבר אמרנו באות י"ג שצורה זו של הגוף שלנו שהוא הרצון לקבל אך לעצמו, אינה נמצאת כלל במחשבת הבריאה הנצחית, כי שם אנו עומדים בצורתנו של מצב הג'. אלא שהיא מחויבת לנו במציאות הב' כדי לאפשר לנו לתקנה כנ"ל.

ואין לשאול כלל על מצב שאר בריות העולם חוץ מהאדם. משום שהאדם הוא מרכז כל הבריאה כמ"ש להלן (באות לט), וכל שאר הבריות אין להן חשבון וערך של כלום לעצמן, זולת באותו השיעור שהן מועילות לאדם להביאו לשלמותו, על כן הנה עולות ויורדות עמו בלי שום חשבון לעצמן.

היסורים

י"ט

ויחד עם זה מבוארת קושיא הד', שהקשינו כיון שמדרך הטוב להטיב, איך ברא מלכתחילה בריות שתתענינה ותתייסרנה במשך ימי חייהן. כי כאמור כל אלו היסורין מתחייבים ממצב הא' שלנו, שנצחיותנו השלמה אשר שם המקובלת ממצב הג' העתיד לבוא, מכריחה אותנו ללכת או בדרך תורה או בדרך יסורין,

body does not hurt us at all, since it will eventually die and be removed. Our bodies are prepared for us only to the extent necessary for them to [eventually] be removed so that we can receive our eternal form.

ETERNAL CREATURES

18

This also answers our fifth inquiry. We asked: How is it possible that from the Eternal will emerge transient creatures that come into being and cease to be? The answer to this question is now clear. For we emerged from before Him in a manner that is appropriate for His eternality; [we emerged] as eternal and entirely perfect creatures. This eternality necessarily requires that the husk of the body, which was given to us only for service [of God], be temporary and cease to be. For had it [the body] remained in eternality, God forbid, then we would remain eternally separate from the Life-Force of the Living. We have already stated (see 13 above) that this form of our bodies, the selfish desire to receive, is not at all present in the eternal plan for creation. There [in the eternal], we have the [perfected] forms of the third stage. Still, we must exist in the second form [for a time] in order to enable the repair, as discussed.

Do not ask at all about creatures in the world other than humans. For humans are the center of creation, as we will discuss later in chapter 39. The rest of the creatures are not at all valuable in themselves, except to the extent that they contribute to humanity by bringing [people] to perfection. Hence, they [other creatures] rise and fall with him [man], and they are insignificant in themselves.

SUFFERING

19

The above also answers inquiry four. We had asked: It is the nature of the good to be benevolent. If so, why did God intentionally create creatures who would suffer throughout their lives? The answer is that all of the suffering is necessary due to the first stage. The perfect eternality there [in the first stage] depends on the future third stage. This forces one to walk either on the path of Torah or the path of suffering [in the

ולבוא ולהגיע לנצחיותנו שבמצב הג׳ (כנ״ל באות טו). וכל אלו היסורין אינם שורים רק על קליפת הגוף שלנו הזו, שלא נבראה אלא למיתה וקבורה. שזה מלמד אותנו, שהרצון לקבל לעצמו שבו לא נברא אלא רק למחותו ולהעבירו מהעולם ולהפכו לרצון להשפיע, והיסורים שאנו סובלים אינם אלא גילויים לגלות האפסיות וההזק הרובץ עליו.

ובוא וראה, בעת שכל בני העולם יסכימו פה אחד לבטל ולבער את הרצון לקבל לעצמם שבהם, ולא יהיה להם שום רצון אלא להשפיע לחבריהם – אז היו מתבטלים כל הדאגות וכל המזיקים מהארץ, וכל אחד היה בטוח בחיים בריאים ושלמים. שהרי כל אחד מאתנו היה לו עולם גדול שידאג בעדו וימלא את צרכיו. אמנם בזמן שכל אחד אין לו אלא הרצון לקבל לעצמו, מכאן כל הדאגות היסורים המלחמות והשחיטות שאין לנו מפלט מהם, שהם מחלישים גופנו בכל מיני מחלות ומכאובים.

והנך מוצא שכל אלו היסורים המצויים בעולמנו, אינם אלא גילויים מוצעים לעינינו בכדי לדחוף אותנו לבטל את קליפת הגוף הרעה, ולקבל צורה השלמה של רצון להשפיע. והוא אשר אמרנו, שדרך היסורין בעצמה מסוגלת להביאנו אל צורה הרצויה.

ודע שהמצוות שבין אדם לחברו הן קודמות למצוות שבין אדם למקום. כי ההשפעה לחברו מביאתו להשפיע למקום.

מהותנו

כ׳

ואחר כל המתבאר נפתרה לנו שאלה הא׳, ששאלנו מה מהותנו. כי מהותנו היא כמהות כל הפרטים שבהמציאות, שהיא לא פחות ולא יותר מהרצון לקבל (כנ״ל באות ז). אלא לא כפי שהוא מזדמן לנו עתה במציאות הב׳, שהוא הרצון לקבל אך לעצמו – אלא כפי שעומד וקיים במצב הא׳ בא״ס ב״ה, דהיינו בצורתו הנצחית, שהיא לקבל על מנת להשפיע נחת רוח ליוצרו (כנ״ל באות יג).

second stage] in order to arrive and obtain his eternity in the third stage (see above, chapter 15). All of this suffering impacts only the husk of one's [physical] body, which was created only to die and be buried. This teaches that the selfish desire to receive that is present [in the body] was only created to be erased and removed from the world. It is to be transformed into a desire to give. Our suffering only serves to reveal the insignificance and damage that are present in it [the body].

Note that at a time when all of humanity would unanimously agree to annul and destroy their selfish desire to receive, leaving them with only a desire to give to others, all worries and hazards would be removed from the world. Each person would live a secure, healthy, and perfect life, as the entire world would provide and supply all of his needs. Yet, at a time when each person has a selfish desire to receive, that is the source for unavoidable suffering, wars, and corruption, which weaken our bodies by causing illness and pain.

It follows that all of the suffering in our world is designed to motivate us to destroy the evil husk of the body and to acquire the perfect form of the desire to give. That matches what we said above: the path of suffering can lead us to the desired form.

Know that interpersonal mitzvot [*bein adam leḥavero*] take priority over mitzvot between man and God [*bein adam laMakom*], because causing benefit to one's fellow leads him to cause benefit to God.

OUR ESSENCE

20

Given all of the above, the first inquiry is also answered. We asked: What is our essence? The answer is that our essence is identical to that of the essences of all the particulars in the world, which is none other than the desire to receive (as discussed in chapter 7). Yet, this [desire to receive] is not the way that we imagine it in the second stage, in which it is the selfish desire to receive. Instead, it [the desire to receive] is in the way that things are in the first stage, within the *Ein Sof*. That is, it [the desire to receive] has its eternal form, in which it receives in order to give satisfaction to the Creator (see chapter 13).

ואע״פ שעוד לא הגענו בפועל למצב הג׳, ועדיין אנו ׳מחוסרי זמן׳, מכל מקום אין זה פוגם במשהו בעיקר מהותנו, משום שמצבנו הג׳ מתחייב לנו בהחלט גמור מצד מצב הא׳. לפיכך ׳כל העומד לִגְבּוֹת, כגבוי דָמֵי׳, ו׳מחוסר זמן׳ הנחשב לחסרון, הוא רק במקום שיש ספק של משהו אם ישלים את הצריך להשלים באותו זמן. וכיון שאין לנו שום ספק בזה, הרי זה דומה עלינו כמו שכבר באנו למצב הג׳. ואותו הגוף בצורתו הרעה הניתן לנו כעת, גם הוא אינו פוגם את מהותנו, להיותו הוא וכל קניניו עומדים להתבטל לגמרי יחד עם כל מערכת הטומאה שהיא מקורם, ו׳כל העומד להישרף כשרוף דָמֵי׳ ונחשב כמו שלא היה מעולם.

אמנם הנפש המלובשת בגוף ההוא, שמהותה היא ג״כ בחינת רצון בלבד, אלא רצון להשפיע, שהיא נמשכת לנו ממערכת ד׳ העולמות אבי״ע דקדושה (כנ״ל באות יא) – היא קיימת לנצחיות. כי צורה זו של רצון להשפיע, היא בהשוואת הצורה לחי החיים, ואינה כלל ח״ו בת חילוף. ותשלום הענין הוא להלן מאות ל״ב ואילך.

כ״א

ואל יסור לבך אחר דעת הפילוסופים, האומרים שעצם מהותה של הנפש הוא חומר שכלי, והוייתה באה רק מכוח המושכלות שמשכלת, שמהן מתגדלת והן כל הוייתה. וענין השארת הנפש אחר פטירת הגוף, תלוי לגמרי בשיעור שִׂכְלִיוֹת ומושכלות שקבלה, עד שבהעדר לה המושכלות אין כלל על מה שתחול השארת הנפש. אין זו דעת תורה. גם אינו מקובל כלל על הלב, וכל חי שניסה פעם לקנות שכל, יודע ומרגיש שהשכל הוא קנין ואינו עצם הקונה.

אלא כמבואר, שכל חומר של הבריאה המחודשת, הן חומר של העצמים הרוחניים והן חומר העצמים הגשמיים, אינו לא פחות ולא יותר מבחינת רצון לקבל (ואע״פ שאמרנו שהנפש היא כולה רצון להשפיע. הוא רק מכוח תיקונים

Though we have not arrived yet at the third stage, and we have still not had enough time to develop, this does not detract from our essence. That is because the third stage follows inevitably from the first stage, and [to paraphrase a talmudic principle,] "a debt that stands to be collected is [considered] as if it were already collected." Not having had enough time to develop is only a problem if there is a doubt about whether the process will fully develop to perfection in the time available. And since we have no doubt about that at all, [since developing from stage one, to two, to three is inevitable], it is as if we have already achieved the third stage. The body that was given to us for now, with its problematic form, does not damage our essence, since it [the body] and everything it acquires will be completely eliminated together with the source of impurity. And "anything that will inevitably be burnt is [considered] as if it is already burnt" (Menaḥot 102b) and as if it had never existed.

However, this is not true of the soul enclothed in that body. The essence [of the soul] is the desire not to receive, but to give, which has flowed to us from the system of the four sacred worlds of *ABYA* (see chapter 11). It will exist eternally. For the form of this desire to give is equal in form to the Life-Force of the Living, and it is therefore not temporary. This shall be discussed more fully in chapter 32 and on.

21

Do not pay attention to those philosophers who claim that the essence of the soul is intellectual substance, that it [the soul] is actualized only through the knowledge that it acquires, that it [the soul] grows from knowledge, and knowledge is all of its being. [According to this theory,] the eternity of the soul after death depends entirely on the extent to which the soul has acquired knowledge, and in the absence of knowledge, nothing is left [of the soul] to remain. This is not the Torah's view, and the heart rejects this opinion. Anyone who has ever acquired knowledge knows that it is an external acquisition, not the essence of the one who acquires it.

Rather, as explained, all of the substance of the new creation – whether the substance out of which is made spiritual things or the substance out of which is made physical things – is nothing other than the desire to receive. (We have said that the soul is made up entirely of a desire to give. Yet, that is only due to the repairs that occur

של לבוש אור חוזר המקובל לה מהעולמות העליונים שמשם באה אלינו, שענין לבוש הזה מבואר היטב בפתיחה לחכמת הקבלה (באותיות יד, טו, טז, יט). אמנם עצם מהותה של הנפש היא ג"כ רצון לקבל, ע"ש ותבין זה). וכל ההבחן הניתן לנו להבחין בין עצם לעצם אינו נבחן משום זה רק ברצונו בלבד. כי הרצון שבכל מהות מוליד לו צרכים, והצרכים מולידים לו מחשבות והשכלות בשיעור כזה, כדי להשיג את הצרכים ההם אשר הרצון לקבל מחייב אותם.

כ"ב

וכשם שרצונות בני אדם שונים איש מרעהו, כן צרכיהם ומחשבותיהם והשכלתם שונים זה מזה. למשל: אותם שהרצון לקבל שבהם מוגבל בתאוות בהמיות בלבד, הרי צרכיהם ומחשבותיהם והשכלתם רק בכדי למלאות הרצון הזה בכל מילואו הבהמי. ואע"פ שמשתמשים בשכל ודעת כאדם, מכל-מקום דַיו לעבד להיות כרבו' והוא כשכל בהמי, להיות השכל משועבד ומשמש לרצון הבהמי. ואותם שהרצון לקבל שלהם מתגבר בעיקר בתאוות אנושיות, כגון כבוד ושליטה על אחרים, שאינם מצויים במין הבהמה, הרי כל עיקר צרכיהם ומחשבותיהם והשכלותיהם רק בכדי למלאות להם הרצון ההוא בכל מילואו האפשרי. ואותם שהרצון לקבל שלהם מתגבר בעיקר לקבל מושכלות, הרי כל עיקר צרכיהם ומחשבותיהם והשכלותיהם למלאות להם הרצון הזה בכל מילואו.

ואלו ג' מיני רצונות מצויים על פי רוב בכל מין האדם, אלא שמתמזגים בכל אחד בשיעורים אחרים, ומכאן כל השינויים שבין אדם לאדם. וממידות הגשמיות יש להקיש גם כן למידות העצמים הרוחניים לפי ערכם הרוחני.

כ"ג

באופן שגם נפשות בני אדם הרוחניות, אשר מכוח לבושי אור חוזר שמקבלות מעולמות העליונים שמשם באות, אין להן אלא רצון להשפיע נחת רוח ליוצרן, שהרצון הזה הוא מהות ועצם הנפש כנ"ל – נמצא אחר שמתלבשת הנפש בגוף

when the reflected light is enclothed [in the soul. That light] is received from the upper worlds, from where it comes. I explain the matter of enclothing in my *Petiḥa Leḥokhmat HaKabbala* in chapters 14–16, 19. Still, the essence of the soul remains a desire to receive. See the sources there to understand.) For the thing that distinguishes one example of a thing from another is not its substance, but its will. For the will in every essence produces needs, and those needs produce thoughts and knowledge to the same degree [as the needs]. Then, the creature can [go out and] acquire what it requires to fill its needs.

22

People's desires differ from one another. Similarly, their needs, thoughts, and education differ. For example, there are those who desire to receive only animal desires, and their needs, thoughts, and education are designed to fill those animal wants. Though they use their intellect and knowledge like a human, still, "the slave is like the master." That intellect is therefore an animal-like intellect, since it is enslaved to the animal desires. There are also those whose desire focuses on human wants, such as honor or power over others – wants that animals do not have. Such people will focus their needs, thoughts, and education on those [human] desires to the extent possible. Those whose desire to receive is linked to intellectual understanding will focus their needs, thoughts, and education on fulfilling that desire to the maximum extent.

For the most part, people possess all three kinds of desires to different extents. But the admixture of those different needs differs from person to person. This explains the differences between individuals. People differ from one another physically in ways that are parallel to the way they differ from one another spiritually.

23

The spiritual souls of people have only a desire to grant satisfaction to their Creator, and this comes from the power of the reflected light that they receive from the upper worlds from which they [the souls] come. This desire [to grant satisfaction to the Creator] is the very essence of the soul. It follows that when the soul becomes enclothed in the body,

האדם, היא מולידה בו צרכים ומחשבות והשכלות למלאות הרצון להשפיע שלה בכל מילואו, דהיינו להשפיע נחת רוח ליוצרה כפי מידת גדלו של הרצון שבה.

כ"ד

ובהיות עצם ומהות הגוף רק רצון לקבל לעצמו, וכל מקריו וקנייניו הם מילואים של הרצון לקבל הזה המקולקל, שלא נברא מלכתחילה אלא כדי לבערו ולכלותו מהעולם, בכדי לבוא למצב הג' השלם שבגמר התיקון - על כן הוא בן תמותה, כלה ונפסד, הוא וכל קנייניו עמו, כצל עובר שאינו מניח אחריו כלום.

ובהיות עצם ומהות של הנפש רק רצון להשפיע, וכל מקריה וקנייניה הם מילואים של הרצון להשפיע ההוא, שהוא כבר קיים ועומד במצב הא' הנצחי, וכן במצב הג' העתיד לבוא - לפיכך אינה כלל בת תמותה ובת חילוף, אלא היא וכל קנייניה עמה המה נצחיים חיים וקיימים לעד, ואין ההעדר פועל עליהם כלום בשעת מיתת הגוף. ואדרבה, העדר צורת הגוף המקולקל מחזק אותה ביותר, ותוכל לעלות אז למרומים לגן עדן.

ונתבאר היטב שהשארת הנפש אינה תלויה כלל וכלל במושכלות שקנתה, כדברי הפילוסופים הנ"ל. אלא נצחיותה היא בעצם מהותה בלבד, דהיינו בהרצון להשפיע שהוא מהותה. וענין המושכלות שקנתה הן שכרה ולא עצמותה.

תחיית המתים

כ"ה

ומכאן יצא לנו הפתרון המלא של חקירה ה'. ששאלנו, כיון שהגוף מקולקל כל כך עד שאין הנפש מצויה בכל טהרתה עד שירקב הגוף בעפר, אם כן למה הוא חוזר ועומד לתחיית המתים. וכן על מה שאמרו ז"ל, עתידים המתים להחיות במומם שלא יאמרו אחר הוא.

it [the soul] births within the person the needs, thoughts, and education needed to fully grant that satisfaction to its Creator proportional to its [the soul's] desire.

24

[On the other hand,] the essence of the body is a selfish desire to receive. All of its experiences and everything it acquires fill this defective desire to receive, which was initially created only to be destroyed and eliminated from the world in order to reach the perfect third stage and the end of the repair. That is why [the body] – along with all of its acquisitions – is lowly, mortal, and temporary, like a passing shadow, which leaves nothing after it.

In contrast, the essence of the soul is a desire to give, and all of its experiences and everything it acquires fill this desire to give. It remains eternally in first stage and in the future third stage. It is, therefore, immortal and permanent. It and everything it acquires are eternal, living forever. They are not at all affected by the non-being of the body's death. On the contrary, the absence of the defective body's form [after death] greatly strengthens the soul, allowing it to ascend to the heights of the Garden of Eden.

Thus, it is clear that the eternality of the soul does not at all depend on the knowledge that the soul acquires, as the philosophers had suggested. Rather, the soul's eternality is in its very essence – its essential desire to give. Knowledge that the soul acquires is its reward, not its essence.

RESURRECTION OF THE DEAD

25

This also answers the fifth inquiry. We explained that the body is defective, to the point that a soul cannot reach its complete purity until the body has decomposed. If so, why is the body resurrected? Moreover, the Sages say that the dead will be resurrected with their blemishes, so that others will not say that they are different people.

והענין תבין היטב ממחשבת הבריאה עצמה, דהיינו ממצב הא׳. כי אמרנו, כיון שהמחשבה היתה להנות לנבראיו, הרי הכרח הוא שודאי ברא רצון גדול מופרז עד מאד לקבל כל אותו השפע הטוב שבמחשבת הבריאה. כי התענוג הגדול והרצון לקבל הגדול עולים בקנה אחד (כנ״ל באותיות ו-ז עש״ה). ואמרנו שם, שהרצון לקבל הגדול הזה הוא כל חומר המחודש שברא. מפני שאינו נצרך כלל ליותר מזה כדי לקיים מחשבת הבריאה, ומטבע פועל השלם שאינו פועל דבר מיותר. כעין שאומר בשיר הייחוד (ליום שישי) ״מכל מלאכתך דבר אחד לא שכחת, לא החסרת ולא העדפת״.

גם אמרנו שם (אותיות י-יא), שהרצון לקבל המופרז הזה הוסר לגמרי ממערכת הקדושה וניתן למערכת העולמות דטומאה, שממנה מציאות הגופים וכלכלתם וכל קנייניהם בעולם הזה. עד שהאדם משיג י״ג שנה, שע״י עסק התורה מתחיל להשיג נפש דקדושה, שמתפרנס אז ממערכת העולמות דקדושה לפי מידת גדלה של הנפש דקדושה שהשיג.

גם אמרנו לעיל (אות יד) שבמשך שִׁיתָּא אַלְפֵי שְׁנֵי הניתנים לנו לעבודה בתורה ומצוות, אין שום תיקונים מגיעים מזה אל הגוף, דהיינו לרצון לקבל המופרז שבו. וכל התיקונים הבאים אז על ידי עבודתנו, הם מגיעים רק לנפש, שעולה על ידיהם במדרגות העליונות בקדושה וטהרה, שפירושו רק להגדלת רצון להשפיע הנמשך עם הנפש. ומטעם זה סוף הגוף למות ולהיקבר ולהירקב, כי לא קיבל לעצמו שום תיקון. אכן אי אפשר שישאר כך, כי סוף סוף אם יאבד הרצון לקבל המופרז מהעולם לא תתקיים ח״ו מחשבת הבריאה, דהיינו שיתקבלו כל התענוגים הגדולים אשר חשב להנות לנבראיו. שהרי הרצון לקבל הגדול והתענוג הגדול עולים בקנה אחד, ובשיעור שנתמעט הרצון לקבלו הרי בשיעור ההוא נפחתים התענוג וההנאה מן הקבלה.

The plan of creation itself provides an answer, based on an understanding of the first stage. We had said that the plan [of creation] is to bring pleasure to creatures. It follows, therefore, that God certainly created a great and extreme desire to receive all of the positive influence that is present in the plan of creation. The great pleasure and the desire to receive are linked to one another (above, chapters 6–7). We explained there that this great desire to receive is in fact all that God needed to create. Nothing else was necessary to accomplish the goal of creation, given that it is in the nature of the perfect actor [to act efficiently and] to do no unnecessary actions. As we say in the *Shir HaYiḥud* for Friday: "In all of Your labor, You forgot nothing; You left nothing out and added nothing extra."

We also stated above (chapters 10–11) that the exaggerated desire to receive was removed entirely from the system of sanctity and placed in the system of the worlds of impurity, from which emerge [several things]: the bodies, what those bodies need to live, and anything that they acquire in this world. After a man reaches the age of thirteen, involvement in Torah and mitzvot help him acquire a sanctified soul, which is nourished from the system of holy worlds, in proportion to the sanctified soul that the person has achieved.

We also said above (chapter 14) that no repair occurs to the body – that is, to the exaggerated desire to receive – during the six thousand years [of this world's existence] that are meant for the service of Torah and mitzvot. Whatever repairs a person achieves through that service affect only the soul, which rises along the upward path of sanctity and purity. That expands the desire to give that appears with the soul. For this reason, the body will eventually be buried and decompose, since it was not repaired at all. But it [the body] will not remain in that state [of decomposition], for if the exaggerated desire to receive would be annihilated from the world, the plan of creation would not be fulfilled. That is because [the plan of creation] involves [creatures] receiving all of the great pleasures that God planned to bequeath to them. After all, the great desire to receive and the great pleasure received are proportional to one another, and any diminishment of the desire to receive will diminish the pleasure of receiving.

כ"ו

וכבר אמרנו שמצב הא' מחייב בהחלט את המצב הג' שיֵצא בכל השיעור המלא שבמחשבת הבריאה שבמצב הא', לא יחסר ממנו אף משהו (כנ"ל באות טו). ולפיכך מחייב המצב הא' את תחיית הגופים המתים. כלומר, הרצון לקבל המופרז שלהם שכבר כלה ונפסד ונרקב במציאות הב', מחויב לעמוד לתחייתו מחדש, בכל גודל שיעורו המופרז בלי מצרים כל־שהם. דהיינו, בכל המומים שהיו בו. ואז מתחילה העבודה מחדש, בכדי להפוך הרצון לקבל המופרז הזה - שיהיה רק בשיעור כדי להשפיע.

ואז הרווחנו פי שנים: א) שיש לנו מקום לקבל כל הטוב והנועם והרוך שבמחשבת הבריאה, מכוח שכבר יש לנו גוף המופרז מאד בהרצון לקבל שבו, העולה בקנה אחד עם התענוגים הללו כנ"ל. ב) שמתוך שקבלתנו באופן הזה לא תהיה רק בשיעור להשפיע נחת רוח ליוצרנו, הרי קבלה זו כהשפעה גמורה נחשבת (כנ"ל באות יא), ובאנו גם להשוואת הצורה שהיא הדבקות, שהיא צורתנו במצב הג'. הרי שמצב הא' מחייב את תחיית המתים בהחלט.

כ"ז

אכן לא יתכן שתהיה תחיית המתים אלא קרוב לגמר התיקון, דהיינו בסופה של מציאות הב'. כי אחר שזכינו לשלול את הרצון לקבל המופרז שלנו וקיבלנו את הרצון אך להשפיע, ואחר שזכינו לכל המדרגות הנפלאות שבנפש, המכונות נפש רוח נשמה חיה יחידה, ע"י עבודתנו בשלילת הרצון לקבל הזה - הנה אז הרי כבר באנו לשלמות הגדולה ביותר, עד שאפשר להחיות את הגוף בחזרה בכל הרצון לקבל המופרז שלו, ואין אנו נזוקים עוד ממנו להפרידנו מדבקותנו, ואדרבה, אנו מתגברים עליו ואנו נותנים לו צורת השפעה, כנ"ל.

26

We already stated that the first stage leads inevitably to the third stage; everything in the plan of the initial stage of creation will be fulfilled. Nothing [that was present in the initial plan of creation] shall be omitted [in the third stage] (see chapter 15). Therefore, the first stage necessitates resurrection of deceased bodies. That is to say, the exaggerated desire to receive, which had been destroyed and had decomposed in the second stage, must return to life anew. It will be greater and more significant [when resurrected], with no limits at all. [The resurrected bodies] must even contain their flaws. That way, they can begin their service anew, in order to transform the exaggerated desire to receive, so that it will become an equally sized desire to give.

We have then doubled our benefit. First, we have a place to receive all of the goodness, the pleasure, and the softness in the plan of creation, since we have already had a body [in the second stage] with an exaggerated desire to receive, which leads [in the third stage] to pleasures that are proportional [to the earlier desire to receive], as discussed. Second, our receiving in this manner is only for the purpose of giving satisfaction to our Creator. Hence, this type of receiving is considered complete giving (see chapter 11). This will also equate the forms. That [equation of forms] means binding with God, which is the form of the third stage. Hence, the first stage absolutely requires resurrection of the dead.

27

Resurrection could occur only toward the end of the process of repair, that is to say, at the end of the second stage. [Resurrection can only happen] once we have become worthy of negating our exaggerated desire to receive, and once we have received the desire to give, and after we became worthy of all of the lofty levels of the soul – which are referred to as the *Nefesh*, *Ruaḥ*, *Neshama*, *Ḥaya*, and *Yeḥida* [*NaRaNḤaY*]. Then, due to our service in negating the desire to receive, we will have reached the greatest stage of perfection. Only then will it be possible to replace the body – with its exaggerated desire to receive – and we will not be damaged due to [the body's] ways of separating us from our bond with God. On the contrary! We will overcome it [the body] and we will give it the form of giving, as discussed.

ובאמת כן הוא המנהג בכל מידה רעה פרטית שאנו רוצים להעבירה ממנו. שמתחילה אנו צריכים להסירה לגמרי עד קצה האחרון, שלא ישאר ממנה כלום - ואח"כ אפשר לחזור ולקבלה ולהנהיגה בדרך האמצעית. וכל עוד שלא הסרנו אותה כולה מאתנו, אי אפשר כלל להנהיגה בדרך הרצויה הממוצעת.

כ"ח

וזה שאמרו חז"ל, עתידים המתים להחיות במומם ואח"כ מתרפאים. דהיינו כנ"ל, שמתחילה עומד לתחיה אותו הגוף שהוא הרצון לקבל המופרז בלי מצרים כל־שהם. דהיינו כמו שנתגדל תחת מרכבת העולמות הטומאה מטרם שזכו לטהרו במשהו ע"י תורה ומצוות, שזהו בכל מומו. אז אנו מתחילים בעבודה חדשה, להכניס כל הרצון לקבל המופרז הזה בצורת השפעה כנ"ל. ואז הוא נרפא, כי עתה השיג גם השוואת הצורה.

ואמרו הטעם, שהוא: שלא יאמרו אחר הוא. פירוש, שלא יאמרו עליו שהוא בצורה אחרת מהיותו במחשבת הבריאה, שהרי שם עומד זה הרצון לקבל המופרז מכוון לקבלת כל הטוב שבמחשבת הבריאה. אלא שבינתים ניתן אל הקליפות וניתן לטהרה. אבל סוף כל סוף אסור שיהיה גוף אחר. שאם יהיה בשיעור פחות משהו, הרי הוא כמו אחר לגמרי, ואינו ראוי כלל לכל הטוב שבמחשבת הבריאה כמו שכבר מקבל שם מבחינת מצב הא'. והבן היטב.

תפקידנו

כ"ט

ובכל המתבאר נפתח לנו הפתח ליישב שאלה הב' הנ"ל. דהיינו, מה תפקידנו בשלשלת המציאות הארוכה, שאנו טבעות קטנות הימנה, במשך ימי שני חיינו הקצרים.

The same is true of any personal bad trait of which we want to rid ourselves. At first, we must remove it from ourselves extremely and completely, such that none of it remains. Only later can we accept some of that trait again, directing it toward the middle path. As long as it has not [first] been completely removed from us, we cannot direct it to the proper middle path.

28

This is the meaning of statement of the Sages that in the future, the dead will be resurrected with their blemishes, which will then be healed. As discussed, this means that people will be resurrected with the same body [they once had], including the exaggerated and unrestricted desire to receive. The expression "including their blemishes" refers to the ways in which the body is formed by the system of the worlds of impurity, prior to being purified somewhat through Torah and mitzvot. Only then [after the body is resurrected in an impure state, "with its blemishes,"] will it be healed. Then it will achieve the equation of the forms.

The Sages also said that the reason [for resurrection with blemishes] is so that others will not say that it is another person. This means that people should not say that the [resurrected] person is in a form other than what was part of the plan of creation. For the plan of creation included an exaggerated desire to receive, designed to receive all of the good in the plan of creation. But in the meantime, the body consists of husks and must be purified. In the end, it must be the same body, for if [that resurrected body] included anything less [than the original body], it would actually be a completely different body that is unworthy of all of the good in the plan of creation that had been present in the first stage. Understand this well.

OUR PURPOSE

29

These explanations offer an opportunity to answer inquiry number two. What is our task in the great chain of being, of which we are only a small piece during our short lives?

ותדע שעבודתנו במשך ע' שנותינו מתחלקת לד' חלוקות. חלוקה א' היא: להשיג את הרצון לקבל המופרז בלי מצרים בכל שיעורו המקולקל, מתחת יד מערכת ד' העולמות אבי"ע הטמאים. כי אם לא יהיה בנו הרצון לקבל המקולקל הזה לא נוכל כלל לתקנו, כי אין לך מי שיתקן דבר שאין בו.

ולפיכך לא די אותו שיעור הרצון לקבל המוטבע בגוף ממקור לידתו לאוויר העולם, אלא עוד שמוכרח להיות מרכבה לקליפות הטמאות לא פחות מי"ג שנים, כלומר שהקליפות תהיינה שולטות עליו ותתנה לו מאורותיהן, שהאורות שלהן הולכים ומגדילים את הרצון לקבל שלו. כי המילואים שהקליפות מספקות לרצון לקבל, אינם אלא מרחיבים והולכים את התביעה של הרצון לקבל. למשל: כשנולד, אין לו תאווה אלא לְמָנֶה ולא יותר. אבל כשהסטרא אחרא ממלאת לו המנה, תכף מתרחב הרצון לקבל והוא רוצה מאתים. ואח"כ כשנותנת לו הסטרא אחרא את המילוי מאתים, מיד מתרחב הרצון ורוצה ד' מאות. ואם אינו מתגבר על ידי תורה ומצוות לטהר את הרצון לקבל ולהפכו להשפעה, הרי הרצון לקבל שלו הולך ומתרחב במשך שנות חייו, עד ש'אין אדם מת וחצי תאוותו בידו'.

וזה נבחן שהוא מצוי ברשות הסטרא אחרא והקליפות, שתפקידן להרחיב ולהגדיל את הרצון לקבל שלו ולעשותו מופרז בלי מצרים כל־שהם. דהיינו בכדי להמציא להאדם כל החומר שהוא צריך לעבוד בו ולתקנו.

ל'

חלוקה ב' היא: מי"ג שנים ואילך. שאז ניתן כוח לנקודה שבלב שבו, שהוא סוד אחוריים של הנפש דקדושה, המלובשת בהרצון לקבל שלו מעת לידתו, אלא שאינה מתחלת להתעורר רק אחר י"ג שנים (שהוא מטעם הנ"ל). ואז הוא מתחיל להכנס תחת רשות מערכת העולמות דקדושה, דהיינו בשיעור שהוא עוסק בתורה ומצוות.

ועיקר התפקיד בעת ההיא, הוא להשיג ולהגדיל את הרצון לקבל הרוחני. כי מעת לידתו אין לו רצון לקבל אלא לגשמיות בלבד, ולפיכך אע"פ שהשיג הרצון לקבל המופרז מטרם י"ג שנים, אינו עוד גמר גדלותו של הרצון לקבל.

Know that our service during the seventy years of our lives is to be divided into four stages: First, to acquire the exaggerated and limitless desire to receive, with all of its defectiveness, from the impure system of the four worlds of *ABYA*. For if we did not possess this defective desire to receive, we could not repair it at all, since a person cannot repair what he does not contain.

Therefore, it is not enough to obtain the desire to receive that is inherent in the body of a newborn. We must spend no less than thirteen years to become a chariot to carry the husks of impurity, such that the husks shall rule over us and provide their light for us, since their light encourages the growth of the desire to receive. The husks expand the desire to receive, which grows. For example, a newborn wants only a small amount, but when the Other Side grants him that small amount, the desire to receive expands and he wants a large amount. When the Other Side grants him that large amount, the desire to receive expands further and wants even more. If a person does not overcome this through Torah and mitzvot, which help the person purify the desire to receive and transform it into a desire to give, the desire to receive will continue to expand over the person's entire life, to the point that "a person dies with only half of what he desired" (*Kohelet Rabba* 1:13).

The Other Side and the husks have the task of expanding a person's desire to receive, turning it into something exaggerated and boundless. This creates for a person all of the material he needs to work on and repair.

30

The second stage involves the years after thirteen. At that time, there is a "point" [*nekuda*] in the heart, and [that point] is the secret of the "back" [*aḥorayim*] of the sacred soul. That point is enclothed in the inborn desire to receive, but it only awakens after the age of thirteen (for the reasons discussed above). At that time, it [the point] begins to enter into the territory of the system of the worlds of sanctity, at least to the extent that the person is involved in Torah and mitzvot.

During that time, the primary task is to acquire and expand the spiritual desire to receive. From the moment of birth, the person desires to receive only materiality. Thus, even though he acquires the exaggerated desire to receive prior to thirteen years of age, the desire to receive had

ועיקר גדלות הרצון לקבל מצוירת רק ברוחניות. כי למשל מטרם י״ג שנים חשק הרצון לקבל שלו לבלוע כל העושר והכבוד שבעולם הזה הגשמי, אשר גלוי לכל, שהוא בעדו עולם שאינו נצחי, המצוי לכל אחד רק כצל עובר חלף ואינו. משא״כ כשמשיג הרצון לקבל המופרז הרוחני, הרי אז הוא רוצה לבלוע להנאתו כל הטוב והעושר שבעולם הבא הנצחי, שהוא בעדו קניין עדי עד לנצחיות. הרי שעיקר הרצון לקבל המופרז אינו נגמר אלא ברצון לקבל רוחניות.

ל״א

וזה שאמרו בתקונים (זוהר, תקונים חדשים צו ע״ב) על הכתוב ״ולעלוקה שתי בנות הב הב״. שעלוקה פירושו גיהנם, והרשעים הנלכדים בגיהנם זה, צַוְחִין כְּכַלְבָּא הַב הַב (צווחים ככלב ׳הב הב׳). דהיינו, הַב לָן עוּתְרָא דְּעָלְמָא דֵּין, הַב לָן עוּתְרָא דְּעָלְמָא דְּאָתֵי (תן לנו עשרו של העולם הזה, תן לנו עשרו של העולם הבא).

ועם כל זה היא מדרגה חשובה לאין ערך יותר מהראשונה. כי מלבד שמשיג שיעור הגדלות האמיתית של הרצון לקבל וניתן לו לעבודה כל החומר כולו שהוא צריך, הנה היא המדרגה המביאתו לשמה. כמו שאמרו חז״ל (פסחים נ, ב): ״לעולם יעסוק אדם בתורה ומצוות שלא לשמה, שמתוך שלא לשמה בא לשמה״. ועל כן נבחנת המדרגה הזו הבאה לאחר י״ג שנה לבחינת קדושה. והיא סוד השפחה דקדושה, המשמשת לגבירתה שהיא סוד השכינה הקדושה. כי השפחה מביאתו לשמה וזוכה להשראת השכינה.

אמנם הוא צריך לעשות כל האמצעים המותאמים שיבוא לשמה. כי אם לא יתאמץ לזה ולא יבוא ח״ו לשמה, הרי הוא נופל בפח השפחה הטמאה, שהיא ה׳לעומת׳ דשפחה דקדושה, שענינה לבלבל את האדם, שהלא לשמה לא יביאהו לשמה. ועליה נאמר (משלי ל, כג): ״ושפחה כי תירש גבירתה״. כי לא תניחהו לאדם להתקרב אל הגבירה שהיא השכינה הקדושה.

not yet grown completely, since the primary desire to receive involves spirituality. For example, prior to thirteen, the person desires to grab [lit. swallow] all of the revealed wealth and honor present in the material world, the temporary world that is like a passing cloud. The same is not true of the exaggerated spiritual desire to receive, which motivates a person to grab and enjoy all of the goodness and the wealth of the eternal World to Come, which is a permanent and unending acquisition. Thus, the exaggerated desire to receive is not completed until [it develops] the desire to receive spiritually.

31

This [reality in the second stage] is explained in *Tikkunei Zohar* (*Tikkunim Ḥadashim* 97b), commenting on the verse, "The leech has two daughters: 'Give' and 'Give'" (Prov. 30:15). The word "leech" refers to *gehinnom*. The evildoers who are trapped there bark like a dog, saying, "*Hav, hav* – Give, give": Give us the wealth of this world; give us the wealth of the World to Come.

Still, [this second stage] is a great deal more advanced than the first one. Not only does a person acquire an understanding of the true greatness of the desire to receive; not only is all of materiality available to [him in order to] perform the service [of God] that he requires; but this is also the stage at which he can acquire [the quality of doing divine service] for its own sake. [As the Talmud explains, Pesaḥim 50b,] "A person should always engage in Torah and mitzvot, even if [he does so] not for their own sake, as through [the performance of mitzvot] not for their own sake, one comes to perform them for their own sake."

That is why this stage, after thirteen years of age, qualifies as holy. This is the secret of the "sacred maidservant who serves her master," which is the secret of the sacred *Shekhina* [Divine Presence; also a term for the lowest *Sefira*]. The maidservant brings the person to the level of "for its own sake" and therefore makes the person worthy of the revelation of the *Shekhina*.

But a person must do everything possible to reach "for its own sake." If he does not make the effort, if he does not reach the level of "for its own sake," he can fall into the trap of the "impure maidservant," who stands in opposition to the holy maidservant. The task of the [impure

והמדרגה הסופית שבחלוקה זו, היא שיתאהב להקב"ה בתאווה גדולה, בדומה לבעל תאווה המתאהב בתאווה גשמית עד שאין התאווה סרה מנגד עיניו כל היום וכל הלילה, ועל דרך שאמר הפייטן (סליחות ליום ב׳ דעשי"ת): "בזכרי בו אינו מניח לי לישון". ואז נאמר עליו (משלי יג, יב): "ועץ חיים תאווה באה". כי ה׳ מדרגות הנשמה הוא סוד עץ החיים, שמהלכו חמש מאות שנה. שכל מדרגה היא בת מאה. דהיינו כי יביאהו לקבל כל אלו ה׳ בחינות נרנח"י (נפש רוח נשמה חיה יחידה) המבוארות בחלוקה הג׳.

ל"ב

חלוקה ג׳ היא: העבודה בתורה ומצוות לשמה, דהיינו על מנת להשפיע ושלא לקבל פרס. שעבודה זו מטהרת את הרצון לקבל לעצמו שבו, ומהפכתו ברצון להשפיע. אשר בשיעורי הטהרה של הרצון לקבל, נעשה ראוי ומוכשר לקבל ה׳ חלקי הנפש הנקראות נרנח"י (להלן באות מג). כי הן עומדות ברצון להשפיע, ולא תוכלנה להתלבש בגופו (כנ"ל באות כג) כל עוד שהרצון לקבל שולט בו, הנמצא עם הנפש בהפכיות הצורה, או אפילו בשינוי צורה. כי ענין התלבשות והשוואת הצורה עולות בקנה אחד (כנ"ל באות יא). ובעת שיזכה שיהיה כולו ברצון להשפיע ולא לצורך עצמו כלום, נמצא שזכה בהשוואת הצורה לנרנח"י שלו העליונים (שהן נמשכות ממקורן בא"ס ב"ה ממצב הא׳ דרך אבי"ע דקדושה), ותכף תמשכנה אליו ותתלבשנה בו בדרך המדרגה.

maidservant] is to confuse a person, such that the "not for its own sake" does not become "for its own sake." That is what the verse in Proverbs means when it states, "The maidservant who displaces her mistress" (Prov. 30:23). For the [impure maidservant] will not allow the person to come close to the mistress, the holy *Shekhina*.

The final level within this stage is coming to love God greatly, comparable to a glutton who becomes infatuated with a material pleasure, such that thoughts of that pleasure stand before his eyes all day and all night. This is what the poet stated: "When I recall Him, I cannot sleep" (*Seliḥot* for the second day of the Ten Days of *Teshuva*). The verse also states: "Fulfilled desire is a Tree of Life" (Prov. 13:12). For the five levels of the soul [*Nefesh*, *Ruaḥ*, *Neshama*, *Ḥaya*, and *Yeḥida*, referred to by the abbreviation *NaRaNḤaY*] are the secret of the Tree of Life, which lasts for five hundred years. Each level is one hundred years. During this time, he can receive all five aspects of the soul. (The five levels will be explained shortly, regarding the third stage.)

32

The third stage is the service of Torah and mitzvot for its own sake – in order to give [benefit to his Creator], rather than to receive a reward. This service purifies the selfish person's desire to receive and transforms it into a desire to give. To the extent that the desire to receive is purified, [the person] becomes worthy of and prepared to receive the five parts of the soul referred to as *NaRaNḤaY* (as discussed below, chapter 43). The [five parts of the soul] want to give, but they cannot become enclothed in the body (see above, chapter 23) while the desire to receive controls the body, since the desire to receive stands in an oppositional relationship to the soul, or at least it [the desire to receive] is different in form [from that of the soul]. For the matters of enclothing and equation of the form work together (above, chapter 11). When a person becomes worthy and he becomes only a desire to give, wanting nothing for himself, he has equated his form with the higher aspects of *NaRaNḤaY*. (The *NaRaNḤaY* extend from their source in the *Ein Sof*, from the situation of unity, through the sanctified worlds of *ABYA*.) They [*NaRaNḤaY*] will flow to him, and will be enclothed in him, one at a time.

חלוקה ד׳ היא: העבודה הנוהגת אחר תחיית המתים. דהיינו שהרצון לקבל, אחר שכבר נעדר לגמרי ע״י מיתה וקבורה, עומד שוב לתחיה ברצון לקבל המופרז הגרוע ביותר. שהוא סוד ״עתידים המתים להחיות במומם״ (כנ״ל באות כח), ואז מהפכים אותו על קבלה בצורת השפעה, כמ״ש שם באורך. אמנם יש יחידי סגולה שניתנה להם עבודה זו גם בחיים חיותם בעולם הזה.

The fourth stage is the service performed after the resurrection of the dead. The desire to receive, which will be completely eliminated through death and burial, is resurrected with the worst kind of exaggerated desire to receive. That is the secret of "the dead are destined to be resurrected with their blemishes" (above, chapter 28). People then transform it [the body] through receiving in the form of giving, as discussed at length. There are rare individuals who perform this service even while living in this world.

פרק ג׳

העולמות והאדם

ל״ג

ועתה נשאר לנו לבאר חקירה הו׳, מה שאמרו חז״ל שכל העולמות העליונים ותחתונים לא נבראו אלא בשביל האדם. שלכאורה תמוה מאוד, שבשביל אדם הקטן שאינו אפילו בערך שערה דקה כלפי המציאות שלפנינו בעולם הזה, ומכל־שכן כלפי העולמות העליונים הרוחניים, יטרח הבורא ית׳ לברוא כל אלו בשבילו. ועוד יותר תמוה, למה לו לאדם כל אלו העולמות הרוחניים האדירים המרובים.

וצריך שתדע, שכל נחת רוח של יוצרנו ית׳ להנות לנבראיו, היא במידה שהנבראים ירגישו אותו ית׳ שהוא המשפיע והוא המהנה אותם, אשר אז יש לו שעשועים גדולים עמהם כאב המשתעשע עם בנו החביב לו, בה במידה שהבן מרגיש ומכיר גדולתו ורוממותו של אביו, ואביו מראה לו כל האוצרות שהכין בשבילו. כמו שאומר הכתוב (ירמיה לא, יט) ״הבן יקיר לי אפרים אם ילד שעשועים כי מִדֵּי דברי בו זכור אזכרנו עוד, על כן המו מעי לו רחם ארחמנו נאום ה׳״. והסתכל היטב בכתוב הזה ותוכל להשכיל ולדעת את השעשועים הגדולים של השי״ת, עם אותם השלמים שזכו להרגישו ולהכיר גדולתו בכל

Part 3

The Worlds and Man

Creation contains a complex, interconnected network of upper and lower worlds, each of which can itself be repaired, thus contributing to the perfection of humans and the repair of creation.

33

We can now answer the sixth inquiry. The Sages state that all of the upper and lower worlds were created only for man. But this is surprising. Man is not even like a hairsbreadth when compared with all of the things we witness in this world. How much more so [is man insignificant] compared to all of the upper, spiritual worlds. Why would God bother creating all of these for man? Moreover, what does man need with all of these multiple and wondrous upper, spiritual worlds?

You must know that God's satisfaction from benefiting His creatures is proportional to the extent that the creatures feel that God is the one giving to them and benefiting them. He is greatly delighted with them [the creatures], like a father who is delighted with his beloved son, to the extent that the son realizes how great and lofty his father is and [to the extent that] his father shows him all of the treasures he has prepared for his son. As the verse states: "Is Ephraim not a precious son to me, a delightful child? Whenever I speak of him, I remember him all the more. Therefore, I long for him inwardly. I will show him great compassion, declares the Lord" (Jer. 31:19). If you examine this verse carefully, you can understand and comprehend God's great delight, as long as those perfected [creatures] are worthy of feeling and appreciating God's greatness in all the ways that He prepared for them. [This is true to the extent that] they maintain a

אותם הדרכים שהכין בעדם, עד שיבוא עמהם ביחס של אב ובנו היקר, כאב עם ילד שעשועים שלו וכו׳ ככל המבואר בכתוב לעיני המשכילים.

ואין להאריך בכגון זה. כי די לנו לדעת אשר בשביל הנחת רוח והשעשועים האלו עם השלמים הללו, היה כדאי לו לברוא את כל העולמות, העליונים ותחתונים יחד, כמו שיתבאר לפנינו.

האדם - תכלית העולמות

ל״ד

ובכדי להכין את בריותיו שתוכלנה להגיע למדרגה הרמה והנישאה הנזכרת, רצה הקב״ה לפעול זה על סדר ד׳ מדרגות המתפתחות אחת מחברתה, הנקראות דומם צומח חי מדבר. והן באמת ד׳ בחינות של הרצון לקבל, שכל עולם ועולם מהעולמות העליונים מתחלק בהן. כי אע״פ שעיקר החפץ הוא בבחי״ד (בחינה ד׳) של הרצון לקבל, אמנם אי אפשר שתתגלה בחי״ד בבת אחת, אלא בכוח ג׳ בחינות הקודמות לה, שהיא מתגלה ומתפתחת בהן ועל ידיהן לאט לאט עד שנשלמה בכל צורתה שבבחי״ד. כמבואר בתע״ס חלק א׳ עמ׳ ה׳ ד״ה וטעם.

ל״ה

והנה בחינה א׳ של הרצון לקבל הנקראת דומם, שהיא תחילת גילוי של הרצון לקבל בעולם הזה הגשמי, אין שם אלא כוח תנועה כולל לכל מין הדומם, אבל בפרטים שלו אין ניכרת לעין שום תנועה. כי הרצון לקבל מוליד צרכים, והצרכים מולידים תנועות מספיקות עד כדי להשיג את הצורך. וכיון שהרצון לקבל הוא במידה מועטת, אינו שולט רק על הכלל כולו בבת אחת, ואין ניכרת שליטתו על הפרטים.

dear father-son relationship, much as a [human] father does with his own delightful son, as explained by this verse to all who understand it.

We need not expand on this. We need only know that it was worth creating all of the worlds, upper and lower (as will be explained), for the sake of the delight and satisfaction [that God has] from these perfected [creatures].

MAN – THE GOAL OF THE WORLDS

34

In order to prepare His creatures to reach that lofty and elevated level, God wanted these actions to occur in four stages that follow one from the other, referred to as inanimate, plants, animals, and human [lit. speaker]. These are indeed four aspects of the desire to receive, and the upper worlds are divided into four parallel levels. Even though the ultimate goal is in the fourth level (human), it is not possible for [that goal] to appear immediately in the fourth level. It must first pass through the three previous levels, through which it is revealed and developed slowly, until it is perfected in the fourth level. (This is explained in my *Talmud Eser Sefirot*, Section 1, p. 5, s.v. *vetaam.*)

35

The first stage of the desire to receive is called "inanimate." This is the beginning of the revelation of the desire to receive in this physical world. It contains only the general potential for motion that is present in each kind of inanimate object. But we do not see actual motion in the particular [inanimate objects, but only in the species of inanimate objects]. For the desire to receive begets needs, and needs beget the motions necessary to fulfill the needs. And since the desire to receive is small [in inanimate objects], it [the desire to receive] dominates only the general category at once, but its domination over each individual instance is not recognizable.

ל"ו

נוסף עליו הצומח, שהוא בחינה ב׳ של הרצון לקבל, שמידתו כבר גדולה יותר ממידתו שבדומם והרצון לקבל שבו שולט בכל פרט ופרט מהפרטים שלו. כי כל פרט יש לו תנועה פרטית לעצמו, שמתפשט לארכו ולרחבו ומתנועע למקום זריחת השמש, וכן ניכר בהם ענין של אכילה ושתיה והוצאת הפסולת, לכל פרט ופרט. ועם כל זה עוד לא נמצא בהם הרגש חפשי פרטי לכל אחד.

ל"ז

נוסף עליו מין החי, שהוא בחינה ג׳ של הרצון לקבל ומידתו כבר נשלמה במידה מרובה, שהרצון לקבל הזה כבר מוליד בכל פרט ופרט הרגש חפשי פרטי, שהוא החיים המיוחדים לכל פרט באופן משונה מחברו. אמנם עדיין אין בהם הרגש זולתו, והיינו שאין בהם שום הכנה להצטער בצרת חברו או לשמוח בשמחת חברו וכדומה.

ל"ח

נוסף על כולם מין האדם, שהוא בחינה ד׳ של הרצון לקבל, והוא כבר במידתו השלמה הסופית, הרי הרצון לקבל שבו פועל בו גם הרגש זולתו.

ואם תרצה לידע בדיוק נמרץ כמה הוא ההפרש מבחי"ג של הרצון לקבל שבמין החי, עד הבחי"ד של הרצון לקבל שבמין האדם. אומר לך, שהוא כמו ערך בריה אחת של המציאות כלפי כל המציאות כולה. כי הרצון לקבל שבמין החי החסר מהרגש זולתו, לא יוכל להוליד חסרונות וצרכים אליו רק בשיעור המוטבע באותה הבריה בלבדה. משא"כ האדם שיש לו גם הרגש זולתו, נמצא חסר גם בכל מה שיש לזולתו ומתמלא קנאה לרכוש לו כל הישות שנמצאת בזולתו, ו׳יש לו מנה רוצה מאתים׳, וכן נמצאים חסרונותיו וצרכיו הולכים ומתרבים עד שהוא רוצה לבלוע כל הישות שבעולם כולו.

36

Above that is the "plant" aspect, the second aspect of the desire to receive. It is a greater aspect than that of the inanimate, and the desire to receive dominates each and every individual [not just the species]. Each individual [plant] moves independently, as it spreads out near and far to follow the sun. Individual [plants] also have the need for food and drink, as well as the need to excrete. Still, they do not contain individual feelings.

37

Above that is the "animal" element, the third aspect of the desire to receive. It is almost completely present [in this stage], for the desire to receive begets unique feelings in each individual. This is the distinct life-force present in each individual, which makes one individual different from others. Still, they do not possess empathy for others, in that they have no ability to appreciate the suffering of another or enjoy the happiness of another.

38

Above that is the "human" element, which contains the fourth aspect of the desire to receive. That is the highest level of perfection, in that it includes an element of empathy.

I will explain precisely the difference between the third element of the desire to receive, present in animals, and the fourth element, present in humans. It is like the difference between one specific creature and all of the creatures as a whole. For the desire to receive present in animals lacks empathy, and it creates wants and needs only to the extent necessary for that particular creature. Humans are different in that they are capable of empathy. [A human] can feel when someone else lacks something, and he can become extremely jealous of that which another has. If a person has one hundred, he wants two hundred. His wants and needs grow to the point that he wants to grab the entire universe.

ל"ט

ואחר שנתבאר שכל התכלית הנרצה להבורא ית' מכל הבריאה אשר ברא היא להנות לנבראיו, בכדי שיכירו אמיתיותו וגדולתו ויקבלו ממנו כל הטוב והנועם שהכין בעדם, ובשיעור המבואר בכתוב "הבן יקיר לי אפרים אם ילד שעשועים" וכו' – הנך מוצא בבירור שהתכלית הזו לא תחול, לא על הדוממים והכדורים הגדולים כמו הארץ והירח והשמש, ולו יהיה זהרם ומידתם כמה שיהיה, ולא על מין הצומח ולא על מין החי – שהרי חסרים מהרגש זולתם אפילו מבני מינם הדומים להם, ואיך יחול עליהם ההרגש האלקי והטבתו. אלא רק מין האדם בלבדו, אחר שכבר יש בהם ההכנה של הרגש זולתו כלפי בני מינם הדומים להם, הנה אחר העבודה בתורה ומצוות, שמהפכים הרצון לקבל שלהם לרצון להשפיע ובאים בהשוואת הצורה ליוצרם, אז מקבלים כל המדרגות שהוכנו להם בעולמות העליונים, הנקראות נרנח"י, שבזה נעשו מוכשרים לקבל את התכלית שבמחשבת הבריאה. הרי שתכלית כוונת הבריאה של כל העולמות לא היתה אלא בשביל האדם.

מ'

ויודע אני שאין דבר זה מקובל כלל על דעת חלק מן הפילוסופים, ואינם יכולים להסכים אשר האדם השפל והאפסי בעיניהם, יהיה המרכז של כל הבריאה הגדולה והנישאה. אבל הם דומים כאותה התולעת שנולדה תוך הצנון, והיא יושבת שם וחושבת שכל עולמו של הקב"ה הוא כל כך מר וכל כך חשוך וכל כך קטן, כמידת הצנון שהיא נולדה בו. אבל ברגע שבקעה את קליפת הצנון וחוטפת מבט מבחוץ לצנון, היא תמהה ואומרת: "אני חשבתי שכל העולם הוא כמידת הצנון שנולדתי בו, ועתה אני רואה לפני עולם גדול נאור אדיר ויפה להפליא".

כן אותם המשוקעים בקליפת הרצון לקבל שלהם שבה נולדו, ולא ניסו לקבל התבלינים המיוחדים, שהם תורה ומצוות מעשיות, המסוגלים לבקוע קליפה קשה הזו ולהפכה לרצון להשפיע נחת רוח ליוצרו – ודאי הוא שהם מוכרחים להחליט על אפסותם וריקנותם, כמו שהם באמת, ולא יוכלו להעלות על הדעת שכל המציאות הגדולה הזו לא נבראה אלא בשבילם. אכן אם היו

39

It has been made clear that God's entire purpose in creating the universe is to give pleasure to His creatures. That is, they will recognize the truths of God and His greatness and will receive from Him all of the good and the pleasantness that He has prepared for them, as explained based on the verse, "Is Ephraim not a precious son to me?" Therefore, it is equally clear that inanimate objects cannot achieve this goal. Neither can celestial bodies (no matter how brilliant and large), plants, or even animals. All of these lack empathy, even for creatures that are similar to themselves. How could they appreciate God's gifts and His goodness? Only humans [can achieve the goal of creation], since they have the potential for empathy toward those who are similar to them – particularly after the service of Torah and mitzvot, which transforms the desire to receive into a desire to give, thereby equating their form with that of their Creator. After that, they receive all of the levels prepared for them in the upper worlds of *NaRaNḤaY*, which prepares them to receive the goals embedded in the plan of creation. In short, man is the purpose of the creation of all the worlds.

40

I know that many philosophers disagree. They reject the idea that a lowly and insignificant human (in their eyes) is the center of the great and lofty creation. These philosophers are comparable to a worm growing inside a radish, believing that God's world is bitter, dark, and small, like the radish into which the worm was born. As soon as it leaves the skin of the radish and glances outside of it, the shocked worm says: "I thought that the entire world was like the radish into which I was born, and now I see such a great, light, wondrous, and beautiful world."

By analogy, think of those who are embedded in the husk of their inborn desire to receive. They never attempt to obtain the special "spices" of Torah and practical mitzvot, which are capable of breaking through the hard husk and transforming them into a desire to give satisfaction to the Creator. They are the ones who feel compelled to claim that humans are worthless and nothing – for that is what they truly are. They cannot even consider the possibility that all of creation is for their sake. Were they

עוסקים בתורה ומצוות להשפיע נחת רוח ליוצרם בכל הטהרה הנאותה, והיו באים לבקוע קליפת הרצון לקבל שנולדו בה ויקבלו הרצון להשפיע, הלא תיכף היו עיניהם נפתחות לראות ולהשיג את עצמם ואת כל המדרגות של החכמה והתבונה והדעת הבהירה, החמודות והנעימות עד לכלות נפש, שהוכנו להם בעולמות הרוחניים. ואז היו אומרים בעצמם מה שאמרו חז"ל (ברכות נח, א): "אורח טוב מה הוא אומר, כל מה שטרח בעל הבית לא טרח אלא בשבילי".

העולמות

מ"א

עדיין נשאר לבאר, סוף סוף למה לו לאדם כל אלו עולמות העליונים שברא ית' בשבילו, ואיזה צורך יש לו לאדם בהם.

וצריך שתדע שמציאות כל העולמות נחלקת לה' עולמות בדרך כלל, ונקראים: א) אדם קדמון. ב) אצילות. ג) בריאה. ד) יצירה. ה) עשיה. אמנם בכל אחד מהם יש פרטים עד אין קץ. והם בחינת ה' הספירות כח"ב תו"מ (כתר חכמה בינה תפארת ומלכות). כי עולם א"ק (אדם קדמון) הוא כתר, ועולם האצילות הוא חכמה, ועולם הבריאה הוא בינה, ועולם היצירה הוא תפארת, ועולם העשיה הוא מלכות. והאורות המלובשים באלו ה' העולמות נקראים יחנר"נ (יחידה חיה נשמה רוח נפש). שאור היחידה מאיר בעולם אדם קדמון, ואור החיה בעולם אצילות, ואור הנשמה בעולם הבריאה, ואור הרוח בעולם היצירה, ואור הנפש בעולם עשיה.

dedicated to Torah and mitzvot in order to give satisfaction to their Creator with all of the proper purity, they would be able to break through the husk of the inborn desire to receive and replace it with a desire to give. Immediately, their eyes would be opened. They would see and appreciate themselves and all of the lofty levels of clear wisdom, understanding, and knowledge, which are soul-endingly beautiful and pleasant and which are prepared for them in the spiritual worlds. Then they would themselves agree with the statement of the Sages: "A good guest, what does he say? How much effort did the host expend on my behalf" (Berakhot 58a).

THE WORLDS

41

A question remains. In the end, why does man need these upper worlds that God has created for him?

Know that the existence of all the world is generally divided into five parts: 1. *Adam Kadmon* [Primordial Man]; 2. *Atzilut* [Emanation]; 3. *Beria* [Creation]; 4. *Yetzira* [Formation]; 5. *Asiya* [Action]. Each one of these worlds contains infinite details. They are aspects of the five *Sefirot*, "*KaḤaV TuM*": *Keter, Ḥokhma, Bina, Tiferet,* and *Malkhut*. That is to say, the world of *Adam Kadmon* is *Keter*; the world of *Atzilut* is *Ḥokhma*; the world of *Beria* is *Bina*; the world of *Yetzira* is *Tiferet*; and the world of *Asiya* is *Malkhut*. The lights that are enclothed in these five worlds are called *YaḤNaRN* (*Yeḥida, Ḥaya, Neshama, Ruaḥ, Nefesh*). The light of *Yeḥida* shines in the world of *Adam Kadmon*; the light of *Ḥaya* shines in the world of *Atzilut*; the light of *Neshama* shines in the world of *Beria*; the light of *Ruaḥ* shines in the world of *Yetzira*; and the light of *Nefesh* shines in the world of *Asiya*.

All of these worlds and everything that they contain are included in the tetragrammaton, the four-letter name of God, and in the tip [*kotzo*] of the letter *yod*. For the first world, *Adam Kadmon*, is incomprehensible [to humans], and is therefore hinted at only in the tip of the *yod* of God's name. Hence, we do not mention it [*Adam Kadmon*] and speak only about four worlds, *ABYA*. The letter *yod* [in the tetragrammaton] is the world of *Atzilut*; the letter *heh* is the world of *Beria*; the letter *vav* is the world of *Yetzira*; and the [second] letter *heh* is the world of *Asiya*.

וכל אלו העולמות וכל אשר בהם, נכללים בהשם הקדוש י״ה ו״ה וקוצו של יוד: כי עולם הא׳ שהוא א״ק אין לנו תפיסה בו, על כן מרומז רק בקוצו של יוד של השם, ועל כן אין אנו מדברים ממנו ואנו מזכירים תמיד רק ד׳ עולמות אבי״ע. הי׳ היא עולם האצילות, ה׳ עולם הבריאה, ו׳ עולם היצירה, ה׳ תתאה היא עולם עשיה.

מ״ב

והנה נתבארו ה׳ העולמות, שהם כוללים כל המציאות הרוחנית הנמשכת מא״ס ב״ה עד עולם הזה. אמנם הם כלולים זה מזה, ויש בכל עולם מהם כללות ה׳ העולמות, שהם ה׳ ספירות כח״ב תו״מ, שבהן מלובשים ה׳ אורות נרנח״י, שהן כנגד ה׳ העולמות כנ״ל.

ומלבד ה׳ הספירות כח״ב תו״מ שבכל עולם ועולם, יש [בכל עולם] גם ד׳ בחינות דצח״מ (דומם צומח חי מדבר) רוחניים. אשר נשמת האדם היא בחינת מְדַבֵּר אשר שם, ובחינת החי היא המלאכים שבאותו עולם, ובחינת הצומח נקראת בשם לבושים, ובחינת הדומם נקראת בשם היכלות. והן נבחנות כמלבישות זו את זו. כי בחינת המדבר, שהיא נשמות בני אדם, מלבישה על ה׳ ספירות כח״ב תו״מ שהן האלקִיות שבאותו עולם (וענין י׳ הספירות שהן אלקיות, יתבאר במבוא לספר הזוהר). ובחינת החי שהיא המלאכים, מלבישה על הנשמות. ו[בחינת] הצומח שהיא הלבושים, מלבישה על המלאכים. ובחינת הדומם שהיא היכלות, מסבבת על כולם.

Worlds of Existence	***Sefirot* (*KaḤaV TuM*)**	**Lights (*YaḤNaRN*)**	**Tetragrammaton**
1. *Adam Kadmon* (Primordial Man)	*Keter*	*Yehida*	tip of the *yod*
2. *Atzilut* (Emanation)	*Ḥokhma*	*Ḥaya*	*yod*
3. *Beria* (Creation)	*Bina*	*Neshama*	*heh*
4. *Yetzira* (Formation)	*Tiferet*	*Ruaḥ*	*vav*
5. *Asiya* (Action)	*Malkhut*	*Nefesh*	*heh*

42

It is now clear that the five worlds include the entirety of the spiritual reality that flows from the Infinite to this world. However, each world is included in the others. Each world contains something of all five, the five *Sefirot* – *KaḤaV TuM,* into which are enclothed five lights of *NaRaNḤaY,* parallel to the five worlds.

In addition to the five *Sefirot* of *KaḤaV TuM* that are present in each world, each world also contains the four spiritual elements: inanimate, plant, animal, and human. The soul of man is the aspect of the human; the animal aspect is the angels in that world; the plant aspect is referred to as the *levushim* [clothing]; and the aspect of the inanimate is referred to as *heikhalot* [chambers]. Their aspects are dressed up in one another. For the human aspect, which is the soul of man, dresses up the five *Sefirot* of *KaḤaV TuM,* which are the divinity in that world. (The matter of the ten *Sefirot* being divine will be clarified in the Preface to the Zohar.) The animal aspect, which is the angels, dresses up the souls. The plant aspect, which are the *levushim,* dresses up the angels. The inanimate aspect, which is *yekholot,* surrounds all of them.

וענין ההתלבשות הזו משוער בענין שהם משמשים זה לזה ומתפתחים זה מזה. כעין שבארנו בדצח"מ הגשמיים שבעולם הזה (לעיל אותיות לה-לח). וכמו שאמרנו שם שג' הבחינות דומם צומח חי לא יצאו בשביל עצמן, אלא רק שתוכל הבחינה ד' להתפתח ולהתעלות על ידיהן, שהיא מין האדם, וע"כ אין תפקידן אלא לשמש את האדם ולהועילו - כן הוא בכל העולמות הרוחניים, אשר הג' בחינות דומם צומח וחי אשר שם, לא יצאו שם אלא כדי לשמש ולהועיל את בחינת המדבר אשר שם, שהיא נשמת האדם. ע"כ נבחן שכולם מלבישים על נשמת האדם, שפירושו לתועלתו.

צורך האדם בעולמות מדרגות נרנח"י

מ"ג

והנה האדם בעת שנולד יש לו תכף בחינת נפש דקדושה. ולא נפש ממש, אלא בחינת אחוריים של הנפש, שפירושו בחינה אחרונה שלה, המכונה מפאת קטנותה בשם נקודה. והיא מלובשת בלב האדם, כלומר בבחינת רצון לקבל שבו המתגלה בעיקרו בלבו של אדם.

ודע הכלל הזה, שכל הנוהג בכלל המציאות כולו נוהג בכל עולם ואפילו בכל חלק קטן שאך אפשר להיפרט שיש באותו עולם. באופן, כמו שיש ה' עולמות בכלל המציאות, שהם ה' ספירות כח"ב תו"מ כנ"ל, כן יש ה' ספירות כח"ב תו"מ בכל עולם ועולם, וכן יש ה' ספירות בכל חלק קטן שבאותו עולם. והנה אמרנו שהעולם הזה נחלק על דצח"מ, והם כנגד ד' הספירות חו"ב תו"מ: כי דומם נגד מלכות, וצומח נגד תפארת, וחי נגד בינה, ומדבר נגד חכמה, והשורש של כולם הוא נגד כתר. אמנם כאמור, שאפילו פרט אחד מכל מין ומין שבדצח"מ יש בו גם כן ד' בחינות דצח"מ. באופן שגם בפרט אחד שבמין המדבר, דהיינו

"Enclothing" means that they serve one another and develop each other, much as we explained regarding the inanimate, plant, animal, and human levels in the physical world (above, chapters 35–38). We explained there that those three aspects – inanimate, plant, and animal – did not emerge for their own sake. They emerged so that the fourth level – human – can develop and ascend through them. That is, the purpose of the first three elements is to serve man and help him ascend. The same is true of the spiritual worlds. The spiritual aspect of inanimate, plant, and animal emerged there [in the spiritual world] in order to serve and benefit the human aspect that is there, the soul of man. In that sense, we understand that all enclothe the soul of man, which means that they exist for its [human] benefit.

MAN'S NEED FOR THE WORLDS AT THE LEVELS OF "*NARANḤAY*"

43

A person is born with an aspect of the soul of sanctity [*nefesh dekedusha*]. This is not a real soul, but the "back" of the soul, its reverse side, which is referred to as a "point" due to its smallness. It is enclothed in a person's heart – that is, in the desire to receive, which exists primarily in a person's heart.

One should know the following rule: Anything that occurs in all of reality occurs in each [specific] world, and even in the smallest describable element of that world. There are five worlds in the totality of things, which are the five *Sefirot* of *Keter, Ḥokhma, Bina, Tiferet,* and *Malkhut* (*KaḤaV TuM,* as mentioned). These same five *Sefirot* are present in each and every world, and there are five *KaḤav TuM Sefirot* even in the smallest part of each world. We also mentioned that the world is divided into inanimate, plant, animal, and human, which correspond to the four *Sefirot* of *Ḥokhma, Bina, Tiferet,* and *Malkhut* (*ḤaV TuM*). Inanimate parallels *Malkhut,* plant parallels *Tiferet,* animal parallels *Bina,* and human parallels *Ḥokhma.* The root of all of them parallels *Keter.* As mentioned, each particular example in each and every type (inanimate, plant, animal, human) also contains an aspect of all four elements. That

אפילו באדם אחד יש בו גם כן דצח״מ, שהם ד׳ חלקי הרצון לקבל שבו, שבהם מלובשת הנקודה מן הנפש דקדושה.

מ״ד

ומטרם י״ג שנה לא יצויר שום גילוי אל הנקודה שבלבו. אלא לאחר י״ג שנה כשמתחיל לעסוק בתורה ומצוות, ואפילו בלי שום כוונה, דהיינו בלי אהבה ויראה כראוי למשמש את המלך, גם אפילו שלא לשמה - מתחילה הנקודה שבלבו להתגדל ולהראות פעולתה. כי ״מצוות אינן צריכות כוונה״, ואפילו המעשים בלי כוונה מסוגלים לטהר את הרצון לקבל שלו, אלא רק בשיעור דרגה הא׳ שבו המכונה דומם. ובשיעור שמטהר חלק הדומם של הרצון לקבל, בשיעור זה הוא הולך ובונה את התרי״ג אברים של הנקודה שבלב, שהיא הדומם דנפש דקדושה.

וכשנשלם בכל תרי״ג מצוות מבחינת המעשה, נשלמו בזה כל תרי״ג אברים של הנקודה שבלב, שהיא הדומם דנפש דקדושה. שרמ״ח איבריה הרוחניים נבנים ע״י קיום רמ״ח מצוות עשה, ושס״ה גידיה הרוחניים נבנים ע״י קיום שס״ה מצוות לא תעשה - עד שנעשית לפרצוף שלם דנפש דקדושה. אז הנפש עולה ומלבשת את ספירת המלכות אשר בעולם העשיה הרוחני, וכל פרטי דומם צומח חי הרוחניים שבעולם ההוא הנמצאים כנגד ספירת המלכות ההיא דעשיה, משמשים ומסייעים את פרצוף הנפש דאדם שעלה שם. דהיינו בשיעור שהנפש מַשְׂכֶּלֶת אותם. שהמושכלות ההן נעשות לה מזון רוחני, הנותן לה כוח להתרבות ולהתגדל עד שתוכל להמשיך אור ספירת המלכות דעשיה בכל השלמות הרצויה ולהאיר בגוף האדם.

ואור השלם ההוא מסייע לו לאדם להוסיף יגיעה בתורה ומצוות ולקבל יתר המדרגות. וכמו שאמרנו שתכף עם לידת גופו של האדם נולדת ומתלבשת בו נקודה מאור הנפש, כן כאן, כשנולד לו פרצוף הנפש דקדושה נולדת עמה גם נקודה ממדרגה העליונה ממנה, דהיינו בחינה אחרונה מאור הרוח דעשיה

is to say, a particular example among the species of human, even one particular human, contains all four types, which are the four aspects of his desire to receive, in which are enclothed the point of the soul of sanctity.

44

Before the age of thirteen, there can be no revelation to that "point" in his heart. After age thirteen, once he begins his involvement with Torah and mitzvot, even if he does so without intention, or without proper intentions – that is, without the love and fear appropriate for one who serves the King – still, the point in his heart begins to grow and display its actions. For "mitzvot do not require proper intention." Therefore, actions done without the proper intention can still purify the desire to receive, if only the first level, referred to as "inanimate." To the extent that he purifies the inanimate aspect of his desire to receive, he builds the 613 limbs in the "point" in his heart, namely the inanimate aspect of his soul of sanctity.

After performing perfectly each of the 613 mitzvot, the 613 "limbs" in the point of the heart – i.e., the inanimate aspect of the soul of sanctity – will also be perfected. The 248 spiritual limbs are built by performance of the 248 positive commandments, and the 365 spiritual ligaments are built through keeping the 365 negative commandments. Eventually, it [the point of the heart] becomes the perfected *Partzuf* [face] of the soul of sanctity. The soul then ascends and enclothes the *Sefira* of *Malkhut*, which is in the spiritual world of *Asiya*. All of the particulars of the spiritual inanimate, plant, and animal aspects in that world, parallel to the *Sefira* of *Malkhut* in *Asiya*, serve and assist the *Partzuf* of the soul of the person who ascended there, to the extent that a person has understood them. That understanding becomes spiritual sustenance, providing the *Sefira* of *Malkhut* of the world of *Asiya* with all of the perfections that are appropriate to enlighten the body of man.

That perfect light assists the person to invest effort in Torah and mitzvot and to ascend to greater heights. As we had said, a person is physically born with points of light from the soul. [Those points] are enclothed within it [the soul]. Similarly, when the *Partzuf* of the soul of sanctity is born, it is born with a point of the next higher level, i.e., the

המתלבשת בפנימיות פרצוף הנפש. וכך היא הדרך בכל המדרגות, שכל מדרגה שנולדת, יוצאת בה תכף בחינה אחרונה ממדרגה העליונה אליה. כי זה כל הקשר בין עליון לתחתון עד רום המעלות. וכך בסגולת נקודה זו שיש בה מהעליונה, היא נעשית מסוגלת לעלות למדרגה העליונה, ואכמ״ל.

מ״ה

ואור הנפש הזה מכונה בשם אור הדומם דקדושה דעולם העשיה. והוא להיותו מכוון נגד הטהרה של חלק הדומם מהרצון לקבל שבגוף האדם כנ״ל. וכן פעולת הארתו ברוחניות דומה לבחי׳ מין הדומם שבגשמיות, שנתבאר לעיל (אות לה) שאין לו תנועה פרטית לחלקיו אלא רק תנועה כוללת מקיפה לכל הפרטים בשווה. כן האור של פרצוף הנפש דעשיה, אע״פ שיש בו תרי״ג אברים, שהם תרי״ג מיני שינוי צורות בדרכי קבלת השפע, מכל מקום אינם ניכרים בו אלו השינויים, אלא רק אור כולל שפעולתו מקיפה את כולם בשווה, בלי הכר הפרטים שבו.

מ״ו

ודע, אע״פ שהספירות הן אלקיות ואין בהן שום שינוי והבדל מראש הכתר שבעולם א״ק עד סוף ספירת המלכות שבעולם עשיה, מכל מקום יש הבדל גדול כלפי המקבלים. כי הספירות נבחנות לאורות וכלים. והאור שבספירות הוא אלקיות גמורה כנ״ל, אבל הכלים הנקראים כח״ב תו״מ שבכל עולם מג׳ עולמות התחתונים הנקראים בריאה יצירה עשיה – אינם בחינת אלקיות, אלא הם בחינת כיסויים המעלימים אור א״ס ב״ה שבתוכם, ומודדים קצבה ושיעור אל הארתו כלפי המקבלים, שכל אחד מהם יקבל רק לפי שיעור הטהרה שבו.

lowest aspect of the light of the spirit of *Asiya*, which is enclothed in the inner parts of the *Partzuf* of the soul. The same is true of all the levels. As each level is born, the lowest aspect of the level above it is also born. That is the link that connects between the higher and lower levels, up to the greatest heights. The unique properties of the point [that the lower level] contains from the level above it enables it to rise to a higher level. I have said enough about this.

45

That light of the soul is called "*domem dekedusha* – the light of the holy inanimate" in the world of *Asiya*. Its goal is to purify the inanimate part of the desire to receive, present in the body of a person, as discussed. It acts to enlighten spiritually, and this is parallel to the aspect of the inanimate in the physical. As explained above in chapter 35, each individual part [on the level of the inanimate aspect] does not move on its own; rather, a general motion motivates all of the particulars as a unit. All of the light of the *Partzuf* of the soul of *Asiya*, even if it has 613 limbs – i.e., the 613 changes in form in the path of receiving the influence – will not show signs of these changes; rather, [the sign will be] a general light that surrounds all of them together, without distinguishing between details.

46

Know that because the *Sefirot* are Divine, there is no difference between the peak of [the highest *Sefira* of] *Keter* in the [highest] world of *Adam Kadmon* and the *Sefira* of *Malkhut* [the lowest *Sefira*] in the world of *Asiya* [the lowest world]. Nevertheless, there is a vast difference from the perspective of the recipients. For the *Sefirot* are perceived as both lights and vessels. The lights in the *Sefirot* are entirely Divine, as discussed. But the vessels, which are the *KaḤaV TuM* in the three lower worlds (*Beria*, *Yetzira*, *Asiya*), are not an aspect of the Divine, but an aspect of a cover which shields the light of *Ein Sof* that is in them [*KaḤAv TuM*]. They [the vessels] measure and allot the proper amount of enlightenment for the recipients. Each recipient receives only the measure appropriate for the person's level of purity.

ומבחינה זו, אע״פ שהאור עצמו אחד הוא, מכל מקום אנו מכנים האורות שבספירות בשם נרנח״י. כי האור מתחלק לפי תכונות הכלים. כי המלכות, היא הכיסוי היותר עב המעלמת על אור א״ס ב״ה, והאור שהיא מעבירה ממנו ית׳ למקבלים הוא רק בשיעור קטן, המיוחס לטהרת הדומם של גוף האדם לבד, וע״כ נק׳ נפש. והכלי דת״ת (תפארת) הוא יותר זך מכלי המלכות, והאור שהוא מעביר מא״ס ב״ה מיוחס לטהרת חלק הצומח דגוף האדם, כי פועל בו יותר מאור הנפש, ונקרא אור הרוח. וכלי דבינה יותר זך מת״ת, והאור שהוא מעביר מא״ס ב״ה מיוחס לטהרת חלק החי שבגוף האדם, שפעולתו גדולה מאד, ונקרא אור הנשמה. והכלי דחכמה זך מכולם, והאור שהוא מעביר מא״ס ב״ה מיוחס לטהרת חלק המדבר שבגוף האדם, ונקרא אור חיה, שלפעולתו אין שיעור. כמו שיתבאר לפנינו.

מ״ז

וכאמור, בפרצוף הנפש שקנה האדם בכוח העסק בתורה ומצוות שלא בכוונה, כבר מלובשת שם נקודה מאור הרוח. ובהתחזק האדם לעסוק בתורה ומצוות בכוונה הרצויה, הולך ומטהר את החלק הצומח מבחינת רצון לקבל שבו, ובשיעור הזה הוא הולך ובונה את הנקודה דרוח לבחינת פרצוף. שע״י רמ״ח מצוות עשה בכוונה מתפשטת הנקודה ברמ״ח אבריה הרוחניים, וע״י קיום שס״ה מצוות לא תעשה מתפשטת הנקודה בשס״ה גידיה. וכשנשלמת בתרי״ג האברים כולם, היא עולה ומלבשת את ספירת התפארת שבעולם העשיה הרוחני, המעבירה לו מא״ס ב״ה אור יותר חשוב, הנק׳ אור הרוח, שהוא מכוון לפי טהרת חלק הצומח שבגוף האדם. וכל פרטי דומם צומח וחי שבעולם עשיה המתייחסים לקומת התפארת, מסייעים לפרצוף הרוח של האדם לקבל האורות מספירת התפארת בכל השלמות, על דרך שנתבאר לעיל באור הנפש, ע״ש.

In that sense, even though there is only one light, we refer to the lights in the *Sefirot* [in plural] as "*NaRaNḤaY*," for the light changes depending on the qualities of the vessels. *Malkhut* is the thickest cover that shields the light of *Ein Sof*, such that only a small measure of light passes through to recipients. This is appropriate to the purity of the inanimate aspect of the human body, which is why it is referred to as *Nefesh*. The vessel of *Tiferet* is purer than that of *Malkhut*. Hence, the light that passes through it from the *Ein Sof* is linked to the purity of the plant aspect in the body of man, which is more active than the light of the *Nefesh* and is called the light of *Ruaḥ*. The vessel of *Bina* is even purer than that of *Tiferet*, and therefore the light that passes through it from the *Ein Sof* is linked to the purity of the animal part of the human body, which performs great actions and is called the light of the *Neshama*. The vessel of *Ḥokhma* is the purest of all. The light that passes through it from the *Ein Sof* is linked to the purity of the human aspect of the body of man, and it is called the light of *Ḥaya*, which has infinite actions, as will be explained.

47

As mentioned, a person acquires a *Partzuf* of *Nefesh* due to his involvement in Torah and mitzvot without proper intention. It is already enclothed there with a point of the light of *Ruaḥ*. As a person becomes stronger in Torah and mitzvot with proper intentions, the plant aspect of his desire to receive becomes purer. He builds the point of *Ruaḥ* into a *Partzuf* to the same extent [that he has become stronger in Torah and mitzvot]. By performing 248 positive commandments with proper intention, the point expands to his 248 spiritual limbs. By keeping the 365 negative commandments, the point expands to his 365 spiritual ligaments. When he perfects himself in all of the 613 limbs, he ascends to enclothe the *Sefira* of *Tiferet* in the spiritual world of *Asiya*, which transfers to him a great light from the *Ein Sof*. That light is called the light of *Ruaḥ*, which is focused on the purity of the vegetative aspect of the person's body. Every detail of the inanimate, plant, and animal aspects in the world of *Asiya* that are linked to the level of *Tiferet* assist the *Partzuf* of *Ruaḥ* in a person to receive the light from the *Sefira* of *Tiferet*, in all its perfection, as we explained earlier in the discussion of the lights of the soul [chapters 41–42].

ומכונה משום זה צומח דקדושה. וכן טבע הארתו כערך צומח הגשמי, שנתבאר לעיל (אות לו), שכבר יש לו שינויי תנועה הניכרים בכל פרט ופרט שבו לפי עצמו. כן אור הצומח הרוחני כבר כוחו גדול להאיר בדרכים מיוחדות לכל אבר ואבר מתרי״ג האברים שבפרצוף הרוח, וכל אחד מהם מראה כוח הפעולה המיוחס לאותו האבר. גם עם יציאת פרצוף הרוח יצאה עמו נקודה של המדרגה העליונה ממנו, דהיינו נקודה של אור הנשמה, שהיא מתלבשת בפנימיותו.

מ״ח

וע״י העסק בסודות התורה ובטעמי מצוות, הוא מטהר חלק החי מהרצון לקבל שבו, ובשיעור הזה הולך ובונה את נקודת הנשמה המלובשת בו ברמ״ח אבריה ושס״ה גידיה. וכשנשלמת בכל בנינה ונעשית פרצוף, אז עולה ומלבשת לספירת הבינה שבעולם העשיה הרוחני, שכלי זה הוא זך ביותר לאין ערך על כלים הראשונים תו״מ (תפארת ומלכות), ועל כן הוא מעביר לו אור גדול מא״ס ב״ה הנקרא אור הנשמה. וכל פרטי דומם צומח חי שבעולם העשיה המיוחסים לקומת הבינה, נמצאים משמשים ומסייעים לפרצוף הנשמה של האדם לקבל אורותיו בשלמות מספירת הבינה, על דרך שנתבאר באור הנפש, ע״ש.

והוא נק׳ גם כן בחינת חי דקדושה, להיותו מכוון נגד טהרת חלק החי שבגוף האדם. וכן טבע הארתו כדרך שנתבאר במין החי הגשמי (לעיל אות לז), שהוא נותן הרגשה פרטית לכל אבר ואבר מתרי״ג אברי הפרצוף, להיות חי ומרגיש בהרגשה חפשית לכל אחד מהם בלי שום התלות בכלל הפרצוף, עד שנבחן שתרי״ג אברים שבו הם תרי״ג פרצופים המיוחדים במיני הארתם, כל אחד לפי דרכו. ומעלת אור הזה על אור הרוח ברוחניות, היא בערך הפרש מין החי כלפי הדומם וצומח בגשמיות. וכן יוצאת נקודה מאור החיה דקדושה (שהיא אור ספירת החכמה) עם יציאת פרצוף הנשמה ומתלבשת בפנימיותו.

[This light is] referred to as the "plant aspect of holiness." The nature of its enlightenment is parallel to a physical plant, as explained above (chapter 36): Each species differs from the other in its motions. Similarly, the light of the spiritual aspect of "plant" has great power to enlighten the special paths for each and every one of the 613 limbs in the *Partzuf* of *Ruaḥ*. Each one of them [the limbs] exemplifies the particular action of that limb. As the *Partzuf* of *Ruaḥ* emerges, a point from a level higher than it [*Ruaḥ*] also emerges. This is the point of the light of *Neshama*, which is enclothed inside it.

48

Through involvement in the secrets of Torah and the reasons for the commandments, a person purifies the animal aspects of his desire to receive. Proportional [to that purification], he builds the point of his *Neshama* that is enclothed in him in the 248 limbs and 365 ligaments. When he becomes perfect in all of these, it [the point] becomes a *Partzuf*. Then, he rises and enclothes the *Sefira* of *Bina* in the spiritual world of *Asiya*. This vessel is infinitely more pure than the first two vessels of *Tiferet* and *Malkhut* (*TuM*), and therefore it [the vessel] transfers to him a great light from *Ein Sof*, which is called the light of *Neshama*. All of the particulars of the inanimate, the plant, and the animal in the world of *Asiya* that are attributed to the level of *Bina* serve and assist in the *Partzuf* of the person's *Neshama*, so that he can perfectly receive the light from the *Sefira* of *Bina*, as we explained in the discussion of the lights of the soul; see the discussion there.

That point is also called the "animal" of holiness, which is focused on purifying the animal aspects of a person's body. The nature of its light is similar to what was explained above regarding the material animal aspect (chapter 37), which grants individual feeling to each and every limb of the 613 limbs of the *Partzuf*. Each [limb] lives and feels freely, without any dependence on the whole *Partzuf*, to the point that his 613 limbs become 613 distinct and enlightened *Partzufim*. That light ascends above the light of the spiritual *Ruaḥ*, much as there is a physical difference between an animal and an inanimate object or plant. Then, a point emerges from the light of the sacred *Ḥaya* (the light of the *Sefira* of *Ḥokhma*) along with the *Partzuf* of *Neshama* and becomes enclosed in its innerness.

מ״ט

ואחר שכבר זכה באור הגדול ההוא הנק׳ אור הנשמה, אשר תרי״ג האברים שבפרצוף ההוא כבר מאירים כל אחד מהם באור שלם ובהיר המיוחד לו, כמו פרצוף מיוחד לעצמו – אז נפתח לו הפתח לעסוק בכל מצוה ומצוה על פי כוונה אמיתית שבה. כי כל אבר של פרצוף הנשמה מאיר לו את דרכי כל מצוה המיוחסים לאותו אבר. ובכוחם הגדול של אורות ההם הוא הולך ומטהר את חלק המדבר שברצון לקבל שלו ומהפכו על רצון להשפיע, ובשיעור הזה הולכת ונבנית הנקודה של אור החיה המלובשת בו, ברמ״ח איבריה ושס״ה גידיה הרוחניים. וכשנשלמת לפרצוף שלם, אז עולה ומלבשת לספירת החכמה שבעולם העשיה הרוחני, אשר כלי הזה אין קץ לזכות שבו. ועל כן הוא מעביר לו אור גדול ועצום מאד מא״ס ב״ה, הנק׳ אור החיה או נשמה לנשמה. וכל הפרטים שבעולם העשיה שהם דומם וצומח וחי, המתייחסים לספירת החכמה, מסייעים לו לקבל אור ספירת החכמה בכל השלמות, על דרך שנתבאר באור הנפש, ע״ש.

וכן נק׳ מדבר דקדושה, להיותו מכוון נגד טהרת חלק המדבר שבגוף האדם. וכן ערכו של האור ההוא באלקיות כערך המדבר שבדצח״מ הגשמיים, דהיינו שקונה הרגש זולתו. באופן ששיעור גדלו של אור ההוא על גודל דצ״ח הרוחניים, כשיעור גדלו של מין המדבר הגשמי על דצ״ח הגשמיים.

ובחינת אור א״ס ב״ה המלובש בפרצוף זה הוא נק׳ אור יחידה.

נ׳

אמנם תדע שכל אלו ה׳ בחינות האורות נרנח״י שנתקבלו מעולם העשיה, אינן אלא בחינת נרנח״י של אור הנפש, ואין בהן עוד מבחינת אור הרוח ולא כלום. כי

49

After the person has already merited this great light, known as the light of *Neshama*, his 613 limbs will each illuminate with a light that is perfect, clear, and distinct to it [the limb], like a unique, individual *Partzuf*. Then, it becomes possible to be involved in each and every mitzva, following its [the mitzva's] proper intention. Each and every limb of the *Partzuf* of the soul [*Neshama*] illuminates the path of the particular mitzva that is linked to that limb. With the great force of those lights, the human aspect of his desire to receive becomes more purified and is transformed into a desire to give. To the extent [that the desire to receive becomes purifies], the point of light of *Ḥaya* that is enclothed in him is built inside the 248 spiritual limbs and 365 spiritual ligaments. When it becomes perfected as a complete *Partzuf*, he then rises to the *Sefira* of *Ḥokhma* within the spiritual world of *Asiya*. This vessel is infinitely pure. Therefore, it [the *Sefira* of *Ḥokhma*] transmits a great and mighty light from the *Ein Sof*, which is called the light of the *Ḥaya* or *Neshama* to *Neshama*. All of the particular things – inanimate, plant, and animal – that are related to the *Sefira* of *Ḥokhma* assist him in receiving the light from the *Sefira* of *Ḥokhma* perfectly, in the way that was explained above regarding the lights of the soul; see there.

This is known as the human [aspect] of holiness, in that it is focused on purifying the human aspect of the body of the person. The quality of that light in the Divine is like the quality of the human in the physical [structure of] inanimate, plant, animal, and human, in that he acquires sympathy for others. The greatness of that [human] spiritual light is greater than the [lights of the] spiritual inanimate, plant, and animal aspects, in the same measure that the physical human aspect is greater than the physical inanimate, plant, and animal aspects.

The aspect of light of the *Ein Sof* that is enclothed in this *Partzuf* is the point of the light of *Yeḥida*.

50

Yet, you should know that each of the five aspects of the lights of *NaRaNḤaY* that are received from the world of *Asiya* are nothing other than the aspects of *NaRanḤaY* of the light of the *Nefesh*. They do not

אין אור הרוח אלא בעולם היצירה, ואור הנשמה רק בעולם הבריאה, ואור החיה רק בעולם אצילות, ואור היחידה רק בעולם א״ק. אלא כמו שאמרנו לעיל, שכל שיש בכלל כולו מתגלה גם כן בכל הפרטים, עד הפרט היותר קטן שאך אפשר להיפרט. ולפיכך יש כל ה׳ בחינות נרנח״י גם בעולם העשיה, כדרך שבארנו אותן, אבל הן רק נרנח״י דנפש. וממש על דרך זה יש כל ה׳ בחינות נרנח״י בעולם היצירה והן רק ה׳ חלקי הרוח. וכן יש כל ה׳ בחינות נרנח״י בעולם הבריאה, והן ה׳ חלקי הנשמה. וכן הוא בעולם האצילות, שהן ה׳ חלקי אור החיה. וכן הוא בעולם א״ק, שהן ה׳ חלקי אור היחידה. וההפרש שבין עולם לעולם, הוא על דרך שבארנו בהבחנות שבין כל אחד מנרנח״י דעשיה.

נ״א

ודע, שהתשובה והטהרה אינה מקובלת זולת שתהיה בקביעות מוחלטת שלא ישוב לכסלו עוד. וזה שאמרו (עי׳ רמב״ם הל׳ תשובה ב, ב): ״היכי דמי תשובה? עד שיעיד עליו יודע תעלומות שלא ישוב לכסלו עוד״. נמצא שמה שאמרנו שאם אדם מטהר את חלק הדומם מהרצון לקבל שבו, שהוא זוכה לפרצוף נפש דעשיה ועולה ומלביש את ספירת המלכות דעשיה, היינו ודאי שיזכה בטהרת חלק הדומם בקביעות מוחלטת באופן שלא ישוב לכסלו עוד. ואז יכול לעלות לעולם העשיה הרוחני, כי יש לו טהרה והשוואת הצורה בהחלט לעולם ההוא. אמנם שאר המדרגות שאמרנו, שהן רוח נשמה חיה יחידה דעשיה, שצריך לטהר כנגדן את חלק הצומח והחי והמדבר מהרצון לקבל שלו שילבישו ויקבלו האורות ההם, אין הטהרה צריכה להיות בקביעות מוחלטת עד שיעיד עליו יודע תעלומות שלא ישוב לכסלו עוד.

retain any element of the light of *Ruaḥ*. For the light of *Ruaḥ* is present only in the world of *Yetzira*; similarly, the light of *Neshama* is present only in the world of *Beria*, the light of *Ḥaya* is only present in the world of *Atzilut*, and the light of *Yeḥida* is only present in the world of *Adam Kadmon*. Rather, as stated above, anything that contains a part of the whole, all of the details [of that whole] are revealed in it as well, down to the smallest imaginable detail. Hence, the world of *Asiya* contains all five elements of the *NaRaNḤaY*, as explained above, but they [the five elements] are only the *NaRaNḤaY* of the *Nefesh*. Similarly, all five elements of the *NaRaNḤaY* are present in the world of *Yetzira*, and they are the five parts of *Ruaḥ*. Again, all five elements of the *NaRaNḤaY* are present in the world of *Beria*, and they are the five parts of the *Neshama*. The same is true of the world of *Atzilut*, which contain the five parts of the light [of *NaRaNḤaY*] of *Ḥaya*. The parallel is also true in the world of *Adam Kadmon*, in which are present the five parts of the light [of *NaRaNḤaY*] of *Yeḥida*. The difference between each world is similar to what we explained when distinguishing between each aspect of the *NaRaNḤaY* of *Asiya*.

51

Know that a person's repentance and purity are not accepted unless it is absolutely clear that that person will not return to his foolishness [sins] in the future. As the Rambam explains (*Hilkhot Teshuva* 2:2): "What constitutes *teshuva* [repentance]?... [He must reach the level at which] He who knows the hidden [God] will testify concerning him that he will never return to this sin again." It follows that if a person purifies the inanimate part of his desire to receive, he becomes worthy of the *Partzuf* of the *Nefesh* of *Asiya*. He ascends and enclothes the *Sefira* of *Malkhut* of *Asiya*. It is certain that he becomes worthy of absolutely, permanently purifying the inanimate part, such that he will never return to his foolishness. Yet, we have spoken of other levels of *Asiya* – *Ruaḥ*, *Neshama*, *Ḥaya*, and *Yeḥida*. Parallel to them, he must purify the plant, animal, and human aspects of his desire to receive, such that they will enclothe and receive their lights. This purification does not need to be absolutely permanent, such that He who knows the hidden will testify that he will not return to his foolishness.

והוא מטעם שכל עולם העשיה בכל ה׳ ספירות כח״ב תו״מ שבו, אינו אלא בחינת מלכות לבד, שיחסה רק לטהרת הדומם בלבד, וה׳ הספירות הן רק ה׳ חלקי המלכות. ועל כן כיון שכבר זכה על כל פנים בטהרת חלק הדומם שברצון לקבל, כבר יש לו השוואת הצורה לכל עולם העשיה. אלא כיון שכל ספירה וספירה מעולם העשיה מקבלת מהבחינה שכנגדה בעולמות העליונים ממנה. למשל: ספירת הת״ת דעשיה מקבלת מעולם היצירה, שכולו בחינת ת״ת ואור הרוח. וספירת בינה דעשיה מקבלת מעולם הבריאה, שכולו בחינת נשמה. וספירת חכמה דעשיה מקבלת מעולם האצילות, שכולו חכמה ואור החיה. ולפיכך אע״פ שלא טיהר אלא חלק הדומם בקביעות, מכל מקום אם טיהר שאר ג׳ חלקי הרצון לקבל שלו, על כל פנים שלא בקביעות, הוא יכול לקבל גם רוח נשמה חיה מת״ת ובינה וחכמה דעשיה, אלא רק שלא בקביעות, כי בשעה שנתעורר שוב אחד מג׳ חלקי הרצון לקבל שלו, נמצא תכף שאיבד את האורות ההם.

נ״ב

ואחר שמטהר גם חלק הצומח שברצון לקבל שלו בבחינת קביעות, הוא עולה לעולם היצירה בקביעות ומשיג שם עד מדרגת הרוח בקביעות. ויכול להשיג שם גם האורות נשמה וחיה מספירות בינה וחכמה אשר שם הנבחנות לנשמה דרוח וחיה דרוח, אפילו מטרם שזכה לטהרת חלק החי והמדבר בבחינת קביעות מוחלטת, על דרך שנתבאר בעולם העשיה. אבל רק שלא בקביעות. כי אחר שהשיג טהרת הצומח מהרצון לקבל שבו בבחינת הקביעות, כבר הוא בהשוואת הצורה לעולם היצירה כולו עד רום המעלות, כנ״ל בעולם העשיה.

נ״ג

ואחר שמטהר גם חלק החי מהרצון לקבל והופכו לרצון להשפיע, עד שיודע תעלומות יעיד עליו שלא ישוב לכסלו עוד, כבר הוא בהשוואת הצורה לעולם הבריאה ועולה ומקבל שם עד אור הנשמה בקביעות. וגם ע״י טהרת חלק המדבר

This is because the entire world of *Asiya,* with the five *Sefirot* of *KaḤaV TuM,* contains only aspects of *Malkhut,* which is parallel only to the purification of the inanimate. These five *Sefirot* are only parts of *Malkhut.* Since he has already purified the inanimate aspect of his desire to receive, he has equated his form with the entire world of *Asiya.* Still, each and every *Sefira* in the world of *Asiya* receives from the parallel aspect of the even higher worlds. For example, the *Sefira* of *Tiferet* of *Asiya* receives from the world of *Yetzira,* which is [itself] all an aspect of *Tiferet* and the light of *Ruaḥ.* The *Sefira* of *Bina* in [the world of] *Asiya* receives from the world of *Beria,* which is entirely an aspect of *Neshama.* And the *Sefira* of *Ḥokhma* of *Asiya* receives from the world of *Atzilut,* which is entirely *Ḥokhma* and the light of *Ḥaya.* Hence, even though the person has only permanently purified his inanimate part, if he purifies the other three parts of his desire to receive, even temporarily, he can still receive *Ruaḥ, Neshama,* and *Ḥaya* from *Tiferet, Bina,* and *Ḥokhma* of *Asiya.* That [reception] will only be temporary, for the moment that one part of his desire to receive awakens, he will immediately lose those lights.

52

After a person permanently purifies the plant parts of his desire to receive, he completely ascends to the world of *Yetzira* and totally acquires the level of *Ruaḥ.* He can also receive there the lights of *Neshama* and *Ḥaya* from the *Sefirot* of *Bina* and *Ḥokhma,* which are defined as *Neshama* of *Ruaḥ* and *Ḥaya* of *Ruaḥ.* This can occur even before he completely and permanently purifies the animal and human aspects, parallel to what was described above regarding the world of *Asiya.* But this is only temporary. After he has permanently purified the plant aspect of his desire to receive, he has an equation of form with the entire world of *Yetzira* at the highest level (parallel to what was described about the world of *Asiya.*)

53

After a person also purifies the animal part of his desire to receive and turns it into a desire to give, to the point that He who knows the hidden testifies about him that he will not return to his foolishness, he then has equation of form with the world of *Beria,* and he ascends and

שבגופו יכול לעלות עד ספירת החכמה ומקבל גם אור החיה אשר שם, אע״פ שעוד לא טיהר אותו בקביעות, כנ״ל ביצירה ועשיה. אבל גם האור מאיר לו שלא בקביעות כנ״ל.

נ״ד

וכשזוכה לטהר בקביעות גם חלק המדבר מהרצון לקבל שבו, אז זוכה להשוואת הצורה לעולם האצילות, ועולה ומקבל שם אור החיה בקביעות. וכשזוכה יותר, זוכה לאור א״ס ואור היחידה המתלבש באור החיה. ואכמ״ל.

נ״ה

והנה נתבאר היטב מה שעמדנו לעיל (באות מא). ששאלנו, למה לו לאדם כל אלו העולמות העליונים שברא השי״ת בשבילו, ואיזה צורך יש לו לאדם בהם. כי עתה תראה שאי אפשר כלל לאדם להגיע לעשיית נחת רוח ליוצרו זולת על ידי סיועם של כל העולמות האלו. כי בשיעור הטהרה של הרצון לקבל שבו הוא משיג האורות והמדרגות של נשמתו הנקראים נרנח״י, וכל מדרגה שמשיג הרי האורות של אותה מדרגה מסייעים לו בטהרתו, וכן עולה במדרגותיו עד שזוכה להגיע אל השעשועים של תכלית הכוונה שבמחשבת הבריאה, כנ״ל (אות לג). וזה שאמרו בזוהר (נח אות סג) על המאמר ״הבא לטהר מסייעין אותו״, ושואל: במה מסייעין אותו? ואומר, שמסייעין אותו ׳בְּנִשְׁמְתָא קַדִּישָׁא׳, ע״ש. כי אי אפשר לבוא לטהרה הרצויה למחשבת הבריאה, זולת ע״י סיוע כל המדרגות נרנח״י של הנשמה, כמבואר.

permanently receives the light of *Neshama*. In addition, by purifying the human aspect of his body, he can ascend to the *Sefira* of *Ḥokhma* and receive the light of *Ḥaya* that is there. [This is true] even if he has not yet permanently purified it [the human aspect of his body], parallel to what was described about the worlds of *Yetzira* and *Asiya*. Yet, that light [of *Neshama*] shines on him permanently.

54

When he then becomes worthy of permanently purifying the human aspect of his desire to receive, he gains the equation of form with the world of *Atzilut*. He ascends and receives permanently the light of *Ḥaya*. When he is even more worthy, he becomes worthy of the light of the *Ein Sof* and the light of *Yeḥida* that is enclothed in the light of *Ḥaya*. This is not the place to expand on this.

55

This explains what we stated above in chapter 41. We had asked: Why does a person require all these upper worlds that God has created for him? What need of his do they fill? Now you can appreciate that a person cannot give satisfaction to his Creator without the assistance of all these upper worlds. For the purity of his own desire to receive is proportional to how much he receives of the lights and levels of his soul, which are called *NaRaNḤaY*. When he achieves each level, he receives assistance in purification from the lights of that level. He ascends level by level until he becomes worthy of the pleasure that is part of the intended goal of creation, as explained in chapter 33. The Zohar explains the talmudic statement: "One who comes to be purified receives assistance" (Yoma 38b). The Zohar asks: What help do they receive? It answers that they receive the "holy soul" [*Nishmeta Kadisha*]. He needs the assistance of each of the five levels of the soul, *NaRaNḤaY*, in order to be properly purified, as included in the plan for creation.

פרק ד׳

הפנימיות וסודות התורה

נ״ו

ויש לדעת שכל אלו נרנח״י שדברנו עד הנה, הרי הם ה׳ חלקים שכל המציאות נחלקת עליהם. אכן כל שיש בכלל כולו, נוהג אפילו בפרט היותר קטן שבמציאות כנ״ל. למשל, אפילו בבחי׳ דומם דעשיה הרוחני בלבדו יש שם להשיג ה׳ בחינות נרנח״י, שיש להם יחס לה׳ בחינות נרנח״י הכוללים. באופן שאי אפשר להשיג אפילו אור הדומם דעשיה, זולת ע״י ד׳ חלקי העבודה הנ״ל.

הפנימיות וסודות התורה באופן שאין לך אדם מישראל שיפטור עצמו מלעסוק בכולן לפי ערכו. והוא צריך לעסוק בתורה ומצוות בכוונה, בכדי לקבל בחי׳ רוח בערכו. והוא צריך לעסוק בסודות התורה לפי ערכו, כדי שיקבל בחי׳ נשמה לפי ערכו, וכן בטעמי מצוות. כי אי אפשר לאור היותר קטן שבמציאות הקדושה שיהיה נשלם זולתם.

Part 4

The Internal and Secret Aspects of Torah

Study and understanding of the secret aspects of Torah, the Kabbala, enable the repair of creation. At this point in history, it is possible and necessary to spread study of Kabbala far and wide.

56

You should realize that all of the *NaRaNḤaY*, of which we have spoken up to now, are in fact five divisions that together make up reality as a whole. For the macro is present in the micro. For example, it is possible [for the individual] to achieve all five aspects of *NaRaNḤaY* – related to the five general aspects of *NaRaNḤaY* – even from the inanimate aspect of the spiritual world of *Asiya*. Similarly, it is impossible to acquire even the light of the inanimate of *Asiya* without [also acquiring] the [other] four aspects of service [of God], as discussed.

The inner meaning and the secrets of Torah are such that it is not possible for a Jew to ignore them; he must be involved with them to the extent that he is capable. He must be involved with Torah and mitzvot with proper intention in order to acquire the aspect of *Ruaḥ* at the appropriate level for him. He must also be involved in the secrets of Torah at the appropriate level so that he can acquire the aspect of *Neshama* at the proper level. The same [is true] regarding [study of] the reasons for the commandments. For even the smallest light in sacred reality cannot be perfected without these areas of study.

סיבת היבשות והחשכות בדורנו

נ"ז

ומכאן תבין את היבשות והחשכות שמצאונו בדורנו זה, שלא נשמע כמוהן בכל הדורות שקדמו לנו. שהוא משום שאפילו העובדי ה' שמטו ידיהם מהעסק בסודות התורה. וכבר המשיל הרמב"ם ז"ל משל אמיתי על זה ואמר, שאם שורה של אלף אנשים סומים הולכים בדרך, ויש להם על כל פנים פיקח אחד בראשם – הרי הם בטוחים כולם שילכו בדרך הישר ולא יפלו בפחים ומכמורות, להיותם נמשכים אחר הפיקח שבראשם. אבל אם חסר להם אותו האחד, בלי ספק שיכשלו בכל דבר המוטל בדרך ויפלו כולם לבור שחת. כן הדבר שלפנינו, אם היו על כל פנים עובדי השי"ת עוסקים בפנימיות התורה, והמשיכו אור שלם מא"ס ב"ה, הרי כל בני הדור היו נמשכים אחריהם וכולם היו בטוחים בדרכם שלא יכשלו. ואם גם עובדי השי"ת סלקו את עצמם מחכמה זו, אין פלא שכל הדור נכשל בגללם. ומגודל צערי לא אוכל להאריך בזה.

הפתרון לחשכות

נ"ח

אמנם ידעתי הסיבה, שהיא בעיקר מתוך שנתמעטה האמונה בכלל והאמונה בקדושי עליון חכמי הדורות בפרט, וספרי הקבלה והזוהר מלאים ממשלים גשמיים – על כן נפל הפחד על כל אחד שלא יצא שכרו בהפסדו, כי ח"ו קרוב להכשל בפסל ודמות.

והוא שהעירני לעשות ביאור מספיק על כתבי האר"י ז"ל, ועתה על הזוהר הקדוש, והסרתי הפחד הזה לגמרי. כי ביארתי והוכחתי בעליל, את הנמשל הרוחני של כל דבר, שהוא מופשט מכל דמיון גשמי, למעלה מהמקום ולמעלה

THE REASON FOR THE DROUGHT AND DARKNESS IN OUR GENERATION

57

Now you can understand the drought and darkness of our generation, which is unlike that of any earlier generation. For even those who continue to serve God have abandoned their involvement in the secrets of Torah. The Rambam has articulated this through an allegory. If there are one thousand blind people walking on a path with one sighted person leading them, then they are sure to remain on the proper path, and they will not trip over obstacles, as the sighted person will lead them. But if there is no sighted person, they will certainly trip over anything in their path and fall into a dangerous pit.

The same is true in this matter. If those who serve God would be involved at all in the inner meaning of Torah, and if they would draw down pure light from the *Ein Sof*, then the rest of the generation could follow them and continue on the path confidently. But if even those who serve God have abandoned this wisdom, it is not surprising that the rest of the generation fails because of them. This is so painful that I cannot say more about it.

THE SOLUTION TO THE DARKNESS

58

I know that the true cause [of the drought and darkness of the generation] is the decline of faith in general, and faith in the holy sages in particular. Kabbalistic books, including the Zohar, are filled with parables of material things. Therefore, people were so afraid of doing more damage than good, since it might lead to sin by believing that there is some corporeality in God [that they stopped teaching the secrets of Torah].

This darkness led me to write a commentary on the works of Rabbi Isaac Luria, the Ari z"l, and later on the holy Zohar. I was able to remove this fear by explaining and demonstrating clearly that these parables are not speaking of something physical, but of something spiritual, something more abstract than anything that can be imagined in the physical world, something above place and time. Those who read [those

מהזמן, כמו שיראו המעיינים, למען לאפשר לכל המון בית ישראל ללמוד ספר הזוהר ולהתחמם באורו הקדוש.

וקראתי הביאור בשם 'הסולם', להורות שתפקיד ביאורי הוא כתפקיד כל סולם. שאם יש לך עליה מלאה כל טוב, אינך חסר אלא סולם לעלות בו, ואז כל טוב העולם בידיך.

אמנם אין הסולם מטרה כלפי עצמו. כי אם תנוח במדרגות הסולם ולא תכנס אל העליה, אז לא תושלם כוונתך. כן הדבר בביאור שלי על הזוהר. כי לבאר דבריהם העמוקים מכל עמוק עד סופם, עוד לא נברא הביטוי לזה. אלא עשיתי על כל פנים בביאורי זה דרך ומבוא לכל בן אדם, שיוכל על ידו לעלות ולהעמיק ולהסתכל בספר הזוהר גופֵיה (עצמו). כי רק אז תושלם כוונתי בביאורי זה.

מחבר ספר הזוהר

נ"ט

והנה כל המצויים אצל ספר הזוהר הקדוש, כלומר המבינים מה שכתוב בו, הסכימו פה אחד שספר הזוהר הקדוש חיברו התנא האלהי רבי שמעון בן יוחאי. חוץ מהרחוקים מחכמה זו, שיש מהם המפקפקים ביחוסו זה ונוטים לומר על סמך מעשיות בדויות ממתנגדי החכמה הזו, שמחברו הוא המקובל ר' משה די ליאון או אחרים הסמוכים לו בזמן.

ס'

ואני כשאני לעצמי, הרי מיום שזכיתי באור השי"ת להתבונן מעט בספר הקדוש הזה לא עלה על לבי לחקור ביחוסו. והוא מטעם פשוט, כי לפי תוכנו של הספר, עלתה בלבי מעלת יקר התנא רשב"י, לאין ערך יותר על כל התנאים הקדושים. ואם היה מתברר לי בבירור גמור שמחברו הוא שם אחר, כגון ר' משה די ליאון ז"ל וכדומה, הרי אז היתה גדלה אצלי מעלת האיש ר"מ די ליאון ז"ל, יותר מכל התנאים הקדושים וגם רשב"י בכללם.

אמנם באמת לפי מידת עומק החכמה שבספר, אם הייתי מוצא בבירור שמחברו הוא אחד ממ"ח הנביאים, היה זה מקובל על לבי ביותר, מליחסו

commentaries] will realize that they can enable every Jew to study the Zohar and be warmed by its holy light.

I titled this commentary *The Ladder* [*HaSulam*], for my commentary functions like a ladder. If an attic is full of treasure, you need only a ladder to ascend, and then all of the good in the world is available to you.

The ladder is not the goal in itself. If you rest on the rungs of the ladder, you will never reach the attic or achieve your goal. The same is true of my commentary on the Zohar. Words are not adequate to fully explain these infinitely deep matters. Yet, in my commentary, I was able to provide a path, an introduction, for all people so that they can ascend and understand the depths of the book of the Zohar itself. That is the real goal of my commentary.

THE AUTHOR OF THE ZOHAR

59

All those who understand the Zohar have agreed unanimously that the book was authored by the holy and divine *Tanna*, Rabbi Shimon bar Yoḥai. Only those who are distant from this wisdom doubt this attribution. Based on imaginary history and opposition to this wisdom, they claim that it [the Zohar] was authored by Rabbi Moshe de Leon or his contemporaries.

60

Speaking personally, from the day the light of God enabled me to begin to study this sacred book, I never considered researching its author, for one simple reason. The content of the book itself testifies to the prominence of the *Tanna* Rabbi Shimon bar Yoḥai, who is greater even than all of the other holy *Tanna'im*. If I were to be convinced that [the Zohar] was authored by someone else, such as Rabbi Moshe de Leon or the like, I would simply come to the conclusion that that person, Rabbi Moshe de Leon, is greater than all of the holy *Tanna'im*, including Rabbi Shimon bar Yoḥai.

Indeed, the book is so deep and wise that evidence that it was written by one of the forty-eight prophets would make more sense than

לאחד מהתנאים. ומכל־שכן אם הייתי מוצא שמשה רבינו קיבל אותו מהר סיני מהשי"ת עצמו – אז היתה שוככת דעתי לגמרי, כי לו נאה ולו יאה חיבור כזה. ולפיכך, כיון שזכיתי לערוך ביאור מספיק השווה לכל בעל עיון, להבין מעט מה שכתוב בו בספר, אני חושב שכבר נפטרתי בזה לגמרי מלטרוח עוד ולהכניס עצמי בחקירה הזאת, כי כל משכיל בזוהר לא יוכל להסתפק עוד שמחברו יוכל להיות איש פחות במעלה מהתנא רשב"י הקדוש.

גילויו בדורות האחרונים

ס"א

אכן לפי זה נשאלת השאלה, למה לא היה נגלה ספר הזוהר לדורות הראשונים, שבלי ספק היו חשובים במעלה יותר מדורות האחרונים והיו ראויים לו יותר. ויחד עם זה יש לשאול, למה לא נגלה ביאור ספר הזוהר עד האריז"ל, ולא למקובלים שקדמו לו. והתמיהה העולה על כולנה, למה לא נגלו ביאור דברי האריז"ל ודברי הזוהר, מימי האריז"ל עד דורנו זה (ועיין בהקדמתי לספר פנים מסבירות על הע"ח באות ח' ד"ה ואיתא, עש"ה). ונשאלת השאלה, הכי אַכְשַׁר דָּרֵי.

והתשובה היא, כי העולם במשך זמן קיומו של שִׁיתָּא אַלְפֵי שְׁנֵי, הוא כמו פרצוף אחד שיש לו ג' שלישים ראש תוך וסוף, דהיינו חב"ד חג"ת נה"י (חכמה בינה דעת, חסד גבורה תפארת, נצח הוד יסוד). וזה שאמרו ז"ל (סנהדרין צז, א): ב' אלפים תֹהו, ב' אלפים תורה, וב' אלפים ימות המשיח. כי בב' אלפים הראשונים שהם בחינת ראש וחב"ד, היו האורות מועטים מאד והיו נחשבים לבחינת ראש בלי גוף, שאין בו אלא אורות דנפש.

כי יש ערך הפכי בין כלים לאורות: כי בכלים הכלל הוא שהכלים הראשונים נגדלים בכל פרצוף מתחילה, ובאורות הוא להיפך, שאורות התחתונים מתלבשים בפרצוף מתחילה. ונמצא כל עוד שאין בכלים רק העליונים לבד, דהיינו כלים דחב"ד, יורדים שם להתלבש רק אורות דנפש, שהם האורות התחתונים ביותר. זה שאמרו על ב' אלפים ראשונים, שהם בבחינת תֹהו.

attributing it to one of the *Tanna'im*. Moreover, if I became convinced that Moses himself received [the Zohar] on Mount Sinai from God Himself, I would be satisfied. This book is worthy of that. Once I was able to prepare this accessible commentary, enabling people to understand what the Zohar says, I no longer feel any obligation to investigate the [identity of the] author. No one who understands the Zohar could doubt that its author is anyone less than the great *Tanna*, the holy Rabbi Shimon bar Yoḥai.

REVELATION IN RECENT GENERATIONS

61

This raises a question: Why was the Zohar not revealed to earlier generations, which were no doubt at a higher level than the later generations and more worthy of it? In addition, why was the [proper] interpretation of the Zohar not revealed until the time of the Ari z"l and not [during the time of] the earlier kabbalists? And the greatest question of all: Why was the [proper] interpretation of the words of the Ari z"l and the Zohar not revealed until this generation? (See *Panim Masbirot*, my commentary on [R. Ḥaim Vital's] *Etz Ḥayyim*, number 8, s.v. *va'ita*.) Could it be that the later generations are better than the earlier ones?

The answer is that during the six thousand years of the world's existence, the world is like one *Partzuf* divided into three parts: the head, the body, and the end. These three parts parallel [the units of three *Sefirot*:] *ḤaBaD* [*Ḥokhma, Bina, Daat*], *ḤaGaT* [*Ḥesed, Gevura, Tiferet*], and *NeHiY* [*Netzaḥ, Hod, Yesod*]. The Sages state [that those six thousand years] are two thousand years of chaos, two thousand years of Torah, and two thousand years of the Messiah (Sanhedrin 97a). This means that during the first two thousand years, [the world will be] like a head without a body, [for the head contains] only the lights of *Nefesh*.

For there is an inverse relationship between vessels and lights. The first vessels grow with each *Partzuf*, starting at the beginning. But the lights are the opposite, for the lower lights are enclothed in the *Partzuf* at the beginning. Hence, if the vessels contain only the upper [levels], namely *ḤaBaD*, then only the lower-most lights, those of *Nefesh*, descend there to be enclothed. That explains the first two thousand years, the years of chaos.

ובב׳ אלפים השניים של העולם שהם בחינת חג״ת דכלים, ירד ונתלבש אור הרוח בעולם. שהוא סוד תורה. על כן אמרו על ב׳ אלפים האמצעים, שהם תורה. וב׳ אלפים האחרונים הם נהי״מ דכלים, ועל כן מתלבש בעולם בזמן ההוא אור דנשמה, שהוא האור היותר גדול, ועל כן הם ימות המשיח.

ס״ב

גם הדרך היא בכל פרצוף פרטי, שבכלים דחב״ד חג״ת עד החזה שלו האורות מכוסים, ואינם מתחילים להאיר חסדים המגולים, שפירושו התגלות הארת חכמה עליונה, אלא מחזה ולמטה, דהיינו בנהי״מ שלו. והיא הסיבה שמטרם התחילו להתגלות הכלים דנהי״מ בפרצוף העולם, שהם ב׳ אלפים האחרונים, היתה חכמת הזוהר בכלל וחכמת הקבלה בפרט מכוסה מן העולם. אלא בזמן האריז״ל, שכבר נתקרב זמן השלמת הכלים שמחזה ולמטה, נתגלתה אז הארת חכמה העליונה בעולם ע״י נשמת האלהי ר׳ יצחק לוריא ז״ל, שהיה מוכן לקבל האור הגדול הזה, ועל כן גילה העיקרים שבספר הזוהר וגם חכמת הקבלה, עד שהעמיד בצד כל הראשונים שקדמוהו.

ועם כל זה, כיון שהכלים האלו עוד לא נשלמו לגמרי (שהוא נפטר בזמן ה׳ אלפים של״ב כנודע), על כן לא היה העולם עוד ראוי שיתגלו דבריו, ולא היו דבריו הקדושים אלא קניין ליחידי סגולה מועטים, שלא ניתנה להם הרשות לגלותם בעולם. וכעת בדורנו זה, אחר שכבר קרובים אנו לגמר ב׳ אלפים האחרונים, לפיכך ניתנה עתה הרשות לגלות דבריו ז״ל ודברי הזוהר בעולם, בשיעור חשוב מאד. באופן שמדורנו זה ואילך יתחילו להתגלות דברי הזוהר בכל פעם יותר ויותר, עד שיתגלה כל השיעור השלם שבחפץ השי״ת.

The second two thousand years are linked to the vessels of *ḤaGaT*, and the light of *Ruaḥ* descends and is enclothed in the world, which is the secret of Torah. That is why the middle two thousand years are called "Torah." The last two thousand years are the vessels of *NaHYM*, when the light of *Neshama* is enclothed in the world. For that is the greatest light, and that is why they are the days of the Messiah.

62

The same is true of each individual *Partzuf*. Regarding the vessels of *ḤaBaD* and *ḤaGaT*, which symbolically reach until the chest, the lights are covered. They only begin to illuminate the revealed *Ḥesed*, i.e., the revelation of the illumination of the supernal *Ḥokhma*, from the chest and down – that is, regarding his vessels of *NaHYM*.

For this reason, prior to the revelation of the vessels of *NaHYM* in the *Partzuf* of the world, namely in the last two thousand [of the world's six thousand] years, the wisdom of the Zohar in general and the wisdom of Kabbala in particular was hidden [lit. covered] in the world. At the time of the Ari z"l, when the time was approaching for the perfecting of the vessels from the chest down, the illumination of the upper *Ḥokhma* was revealed in the world through the soul of the divine Rabbi Isaac Luria, who was able to receive that great light. Hence, he revealed the core principles of the Zohar and the wisdom of Kabbala, setting aside all of the earlier sages.

Even with all of that, those vessels were not completely perfected. (The Ari z"l died in the year 5332 from creation [1572], as is known.) Hence, the world was not yet prepared for the revelation of his words, and his sanctified words could be understood only by a few elite individuals, who were not permitted to publicize them to the world. But in our generation, now that we are nearing the end of the second two thousand years, it is permitted to reveal his [the Ari's] words and the words of the Zohar to the world. This is very important. From our generation and on, the words of the Zohar will be increasingly revealed, until all that God has planned for the complete revelation will be completed.

ס"ג

ולפי זה תבין שבאמת אין קץ לשיעור מעלתם של דורות הראשונים על האחרונים. כי זה הכלל בכל הפרצופין של העולמות ושל הנשמות, אשר כל הזך נברר תחילה אל הפרצוף. ולפיכך נבררו תחילה הכלים דחב"ד מהעולם וכן מהנשמות. ולפיכך היו הנשמות שבב' אלפים הראשונים גבוהות לאין קץ – ועם כל זה לא יכלו לקבל קומת אור שלם, מפאת החסרון של החלקים הנמוכים מהעולם ומהן עצמן, שהם חג"ת נהי"מ כנ"ל.

וכן אח"כ בב' אלפים האמצעים, שנתבררו הכלים דחג"ת אל העולם וכן מן הנשמות, היו הנשמות באמת מבחינת עצמן עוד זכות עד מאוד, כי כלים דחג"ת מעלתם קרובה לחב"ד (כמ"ש בהקסה"ז עמ' ו' ד"ה ומה). ועם כל זה עוד היו האורות מכוסים בעולם, מטעם חסרון הכלים שמחזה ולמטה מהעולם וכן מן הנשמות.

ולפיכך בדורנו זה, שהגם ש[מצד] מהות הנשמות הללו הן הגרועות שבמציאות, כי על כן לא יכלו להתברר לקדושה עד היום – עם כל זה הֵנָּה המשלימות את פרצוף העולם ופרצוף כללות הנשמות מבחינת הכלים, ואין המלאכה נשלמת אלא על ידיהן. כי עתה כשכבר נשלמים הכלים דנה"י ויש עתה כל הכלים ראש תוך וסוף בפרצוף, נמשכות עתה קומות שלמות של האורות בראש תוך וסוף, לכל הכדאים להם, דהיינו נר"ן שלמים כנ"ל. ולפיכך רק עם השתלמותן של הנשמות הנמוכות הללו יכולים האורות העליונים להתגלות ולא מקודם לכן.

ס"ד

ובאמת נמצאת קושיא זו עוד בדברי חז"ל (ברכות כ, א):

> אמר ליה רב פפא לאביי, מאי שנא ראשונים דאתרחיש להו ניסא, ומאי שנא אנן דלא מתרחיש לן ניסא. אי משום תנויי? בשני דרב יהודה כולי תנויי בנזיקין הווה, ואנן קא מתנינן שיתא סדרי. וכי הווה מטי רב יהודה בעוקצין וכו' אמר, הויות דרב ושמואל קא חזינא הכא, ואנן קא מתנינן

63

Now you can understand that earlier generations were at an infinitely greater level than later ones. For that is the principle of all the *Partzufim* of the worlds and the souls. The purer something is, the earlier it is selected for the *Partzuf*. Hence, the vessels of *ḤaBad* were selected first from the world and from the souls. That is why the souls in the first two thousand years were at an infinitely higher level. Yet, they were still unable to receive the level of perfect light, because the lower levels in the world and within themselves, *ḤaGaT NaHYM*, were not completed.

Later, during the second two thousand years, when the vessels of *ḤaGaT* and all the souls were selected from the world, the souls were in fact still very pure, for the vessels of *ḤaGaT* are at a lofty level, close to that of *ḤaBaD* (see the introduction to the Zohar, p. 6, s.v. *uma*). Still, the lights in the world were still covered, due to the lack of vessels from the chest down, both in terms of the world and the souls.

In our generation, the essences of the souls are at the lowest level of all. They could not be selected for sanctity until today. Yet, they still perfect the *Partzuf* of the world and the aspect of vessels of the souls, and only they can complete this task. Now that the vessels of *NaHY* are perfected, all the vessels possess a head, middle, and end in the *Partzuf*. Hence, entire levels of lights flow to the head, middle, and end, to the extent that they are worthy, i.e., perfect *NaRaN*, as discussed. Only with the perfection of these lower vessels can the upper lights be revealed, not before.

64

The Sages asked this very question (Berakhot 20a):

> Rav Pappa said to Abaye: What is different about the earlier generations, for whom miracles occurred, and what is different about us, for whom miracles do not occur? If it is because of Torah study, in the years of Rav Yehuda, all of their learning was confined to the order of Nezikin, while we learn all six orders! Moreover, when Rav Yehuda would reach in tractate Uktzin [which discusses the extent to which the stems of various fruits and vegetables

בעוקצין תליסר מתיבתא. ואילו רב יהודה כי הווה שליף חד מסאניה אתי מטרא, ואנן קא מצערינן נפשין ומצווח קא צווחינן ולית דמשגח בן. אמר ליה, קמאי הוו קא מסרי נפשייהו אקדושת השם וכו׳. עכ״ל עש״ה.

הרי שאע״פ שהן למקשן והן למתרץ היה ברור שהראשונים היו חשובים מהם, מכל־מקום מבחינת התורה והחכמה היו רב פפא ואביי יותר חשובים מהראשונים. הרי מפורש, שאע״פ שהדורות הראשונים חשובים יותר מדורות האחרונים מ[צד] מהות נשמתם עצמם כנ״ל, שהוא מטעם שכל הזך ביותר נברר תחילה לבוא לעולם – מכל־מקום מבחינת חכמת התורה, היא מתגלה יותר ויותר בדורות האחרונים. והוא מטעם שאמרנו, כי מתוך שקומה הכללית הולכת ונשלמת על ידי היותר אחרונים דווקא, לכן נמשכים להם אורות יותר שלמים, אע״פ שמהותם עצמם היא גרועה ביותר.

ס״ה

ואין להקשות לפי זה, א״כ למה אסור לחלוק על הראשונים בתורת הנגלה. הענין הוא, כי במה ששייך להשלמת חלק המעשי מהמצוות – הוא להיפך, שהראשונים נשלמו בהם יותר מהאחרונים. והוא משום שבחינת המעשה נמשכת מהכלים הקדושים של הספירות, וסודות התורה וטעמי המצוה נמשכים מהאורות שבספירות. וכבר ידעת שיש ערך הפוך מהכלים להאורות: שבכלים,

> are considered an integral part of the produce in terms of becoming ritually impure, the halakha that a woman who pickles vegetables in a pot (and some say when he would reach the halakha that olives pickled with their leaves are pure, because after pickling, it is no longer possible to lift it by its leaves, so they are no longer considered part of the fruit), he would find it difficult to understand.] He would say: We see the disputes between Rav and Shmuel here. Yet we, in contrast, learn thirteen versions of Uktzin. But with regard to miracles, after declaring a fast to pray for a drought to end, when Rav Yehuda would remove one of his shoes, the rain would immediately fall, whereas we torment ourselves and cry out and no one notices us. Abaye said to Rav Pappa: The previous generations were wholly dedicated to the sanctification of God's name, while we are not as dedicated to the sanctification of God's name.

According to both the gemara's question and answer, the earlier sages were greater than the later ones. Still, as far as Torah and wisdom are concerned, Rav Pappa and Abaye were more important than the earlier Sages. Thus, it is explicit that the earlier generations are of greater importance in terms of the essence of their souls, because purer things come into the world earlier. Still, greater Torah knowledge comes into the world in later generations, for the reasons discussed above. Since the general level [of the cosmos] grows in perfection over time, the more perfect lights flow through them [the later sages], even though in their essence, they are inferior.

65

Do not raise the following challenge: If so, why may we not disagree with earlier scholars regarding the revealed Torah? The answer is that the opposite [pattern] is true of perfecting the practical aspects of the mitzvot. There, the earlier sages were more perfect than the later ones. That is because the practical aspects [of mitzvot] flow from the holy vessels of the *Sefirot*, while the secrets of Torah and the reasons for the commandments flow from the lights of the *Sefirot*. As you know, there is

העליונים נגדלים מתחילה (כנ"ל אות סב). על כן נשלמו הראשונים בחלק המעשה יותר מהאחרונים. משא"כ באורות, שהתחתונים נכנסים מתחילה, ועל כן נשלמים בהם התחתונים יותר מהראשונים. והבן היטב.

פנימיות וחיצוניות

ס"ו

ודע, שבכל דבר יש פנימיות וחיצוניות. ובכללות העולם נחשבים ישראל זרע אברהם יצחק ויעקב לפנימיות העולם, וע' אומות נחשבים לחיצוניות העולם. וכן בישראל עצמם יש פנימיות, שהם עובדי השי"ת השלמים, וכן יש חיצוניות שאינם מתמסרים לעבודת השי"ת. וכן באומות העולם עצמם, יש פנימיות שהם חסידי אומות העולם, ויש חיצוניות שהם הגסים והמזיקים שבהם וכדומה. וכן בעובדי השי"ת שבבני ישראל, יש פנימיות שהם הזוכים להבין נשמת פנימיות התורה וסודותיה, וחיצוניות שהם אותם שאינם עוסקים אלא בחלק המעשה שבתורה. וכן בכל אדם מישראל, יש בו פנימיות שהיא בחינת ישראל שבו, שהוא סוד הנקודה שבלב, וחיצוניות שהיא בחינת אוה"ע (אומות העולם) שבו, שהיא הגוף עצמו. אלא שאפילו בחי' אוה"ע שבו נחשבים בו כמו גרים. כי להיותם דבוקים על הפנימיות, הם דומים לגרי צדק מאומות העולם שבאו והתדבקו בכלל ישראל.

ס"ז

ובהיות האדם מישראל מגביר ומכבד את בחינת פנימיותו, שהיא בחינת ישראל שבו, על חיצוניותו, שהיא בחינת אוה"ע שבו. דהיינו שנותן רוב טרחתו ויגיעתו להגדיל ולהעלות בחינת פנימיות שבו לתועלת נפשו, וטרחה מועטת בשיעור המוכרח הוא נותן לקיום בחי' אוה"ע שבו, דהיינו לצרכי הגוף, דהיינו כמ"ש (אבות פ"א) "עשה תורתך קבע ומלאכתך עראי" – הנה אז גורם במעשיו,

an inverse relationship between the vessels and the lights. Regarding the vessels, the greater ones develop first (see above, chapter 62). Hence, the earlier sages were more perfect than the later ones regarding the practical. But the opposite is true regarding the lights, where the lower ones develop first. Hence, the lower ones are more perfect than the earlier ones. Understand this well.

INTERNAL AND EXTERNAL

66

Know that everything contains an internal and external aspect. Within the larger world, Israel and the descendants of Abraham, Isaac, and Jacob are considered the internal aspect of the world, while the other nations are considered the external aspect of the world. Even within Israel itself, there is an internal aspect, the perfect servants of God, and the external aspect, those who do not dedicate themselves to service of God. The same is true with the other nations: Their internal aspect is the righteous among the nations, while the external aspect is the vulgar and damaging people and the like. Even among those Jews who serve God, there are those who are internal, in that they are worthy of understanding the internal soul of the Torah and its secrets, and those who are external, who are only involved in the practical aspects of Torah. Even within an individual Jew, there is an internal aspect, the Israel aspect of him, which is the secret of the "point in his heart," and an external aspect, which is like the other nations within him; this is the body itself. Yet, even his aspect of "other nations" is like that of a convert. Since it [the Jewish body] is linked to the internal aspect, it is like a righteous convert, who attaches himself to the people of Israel.

67

A Jewish person may increase and honor his internal aspect – that is, the Israel part of himself – above the external aspect, the aspect of the other nations. He may focus his efforts and energies on increasing and raising his internal aspect for the betterment of his soul, and he may minimize his efforts to maintain the "other nations" aspect within himself, his bodily needs. That is what the mishna in Avot states: "Make your Torah

גם בפנימיות וחיצוניות דכללות העולם, שבני ישראל עולים בשלמותם מעלה מעלה, ואוה"ע שהם החיצוניות שבכללות העולם, יכירו ויחשיבו את ערך בני ישראל.

ואם ח"ו להיפך, שהאדם הפרטי מישראל מגביר ומחשיב את בחינת חיצוניותו, שהיא בחינת אוה"ע שבו, על בחינת ישראל שבו. וכמ"ש (דברים כח, מג) "הגר אשר בקרבך" דהיינו החיצוניות שבו, "יעלה עליך מעלה מעלה". "ואתה" בעצמך, דהיינו הפנימיות שהיא בחינת ישראל שבך, "תרד מטה מטה". אז גורם במעשיו, שגם החיצוניות שבכללות העולם, שהם אוה"ע, עולים מעלה מעלה, ומתגברים על ישראל ומשפילים אותם עד לעפר, ובני ישראל שהם הפנימיות שבעולם ירדו מטה מטה ח"ו.

ס"ח

ואל תתמה על זה שאדם פרטי יגרום במעשיו מעלה או ירידה לכללות העולם. כי זהו חוק ולא יעבור, אשר הכלל והפרט שווים כב' טיפות מים, וכל שנוהג בכלל כולו נוהג גם בפרט. ואדרבה, הפרטים עושים כל מה שבכלל כולו. כי לא יתגלה הכלל אלא לאחר גילוי הפרטים שבו, ולפי מידתם ואיכותם של הפרטים. וודאי שמעשה הפרט לפי ערכו מוריד או מעלה את הכלל כולו.

בְּהַאי חִבּוּרָא יִפְקוּן מִן גָּלוּתָא בְּרַחֲמֵי

ובזה יתבאר לך מה שאיתא (שמובא) בזוהר, שמתוך העסק בספר הזוהר ובחכמת האמת, יזכו לצאת מתוך הגלות לגאולה שלמה (תיקוני זוהר סוף תיקון ו). שלכאורה, מה ענין לימוד הזוהר לגאולתם של ישראל מבין האומות.

ס"ט

ובהמבואר מובן היטב, כי גם התורה יש בה פנימיות וחיצוניות כמו כללות העולם כולו, ולפיכך גם העוסק בתורה יש לו אלו ב' המדרגות. ובהיותו מגביר

fixed and your work temporary." [If he does so,] his actions cause the inner, "Israel" aspect of the world to rise and ascend, while the external, "other nations" aspect of the world will recognize and respect the value of Israel.

God forbid, the opposite could also be the case. An individual Jew can increase and honor his external aspect, the "other nations" aspect within himself, above the "Israel" aspect. As the verse in Deuteronomy states: "The stranger within you," meaning the aspect of "stranger" that is part of or within you, "will rise higher," while the internal, Israel aspect will "descend even further" (Deut. 28:43). His own actions cause the external aspect of the whole world, i.e., the nations of the world, to rise, and they will overcome Israel and humiliate them, [bringing them] down to the ground; Israel, the internal aspect of the world, will be lowered.

68

Do not be surprised that a single person can, through his actions, cause the entire world to ascend or descend. For there is a fixed rule: the macro and the micro are the same, like two drops of water. Anything that occurs at the macro level happens at the micro level. The opposite is also the case. The micro acts upon the entirety of the macro. The macro will not be fully revealed until all of the micro is revealed as well, proportional to the measure and quality of each element in the micro.

"BY STUDYING THIS WORK THEY WILL EXIT THE EXILE WITH MERCY"

This explains a statement in the Zohar (*Tikkunei Zohar,* at the end of *Tikkun* 6), that by being involved in studying the Zohar and the wisdom of [kabbalistic] truth, a person can bring about the end of the exile and the complete redemption. On the surface, why should the study of Zohar influence the redemption of Israel from among the other nations?

69

The answer to that question is now clear. For the Torah also contains an internal and external element, just like the world as a whole. Hence,

טרחתו בפנימיות התורה וסודותיה, נמצא גורם בשיעור הזה שמעלת פנימיות העולם שהם ישראל, תעלה מעלה מעלה על חיצוניות העולם שהם אוה"ע. וכל האומות יודו ויכירו בשבחם של ישראל עליהם, עד שיקוים הכתוב (ישעיה יד, ב) "ולקחום עמים והביאום אל מקומם, והתנחלום בית ישראל על אדמת ה'" וגו'. וכמו כן הכתוב (ישעיה מט, כב) "כה אמר ה' אלהים הנה אשא אל גוים ידי ואל עמים ארים נסי והביאו בניך בחצן ובנתיך על כתף תנשאנה".

אבל אם ח"ו להיפך, שהאדם מישראל משפיל מעלת פנימיות התורה וסודותיה, הדנה בדרכי נשמותינו ומדרגותיהן וכן בחלק השכל וטעמי מצוה, כלפי מעלת חיצוניות התורה הדנה בחלק המעשה בלבד, ואפילו אם עוסק פעם בפנימיות התורה, הריהו מקציב לה שעה מועטת מזמנו בשעה שלא יום ולא לילה, כמו שהיתה ח"ו דבר שאין צורך בו – הוא נמצא גורם בזה להשפיל ולהוריד מטה מטה את פנימיות העולם שהם בני ישראל, ולהגביר את חיצוניות העולם עליהם שהם אוה"ע, וישפילו ויבזו את בני ישראל, ויחשיבו את ישראל כמו שהיו דבר מיותר בעולם ואין לעולם חפץ בהם ח"ו.

ולא עוד אלא גורמים בזה שאפילו החיצוניות שבאוה"ע מתגברת על פנימיות שלהן עצמן. כי הגרועים שבאוה"ע שהם המזיקים ומחריבי העולם, מתגברים ועולים מעלה מעלה על הפנימיות שלהם שהם חסידי אומה"ע. ואז הם עושים כל החורבנות והשחיטות האיומות שבני דורנו היו עדי ראיה להם. השם ישמרנו מכאן ואילך. הרי לעיניך, שגאולת ישראל וכל מעלתם תלויות בלימוד הזוהר ובפנימיות התורה. ולהיפך, כל החורבנות וכל ירידתם של בני ישראל הם מחמת שעזבו את פנימיות התורה, והשפילו מעלתה מטה מטה ועשו אותה כמו שהיתה ח"ו דבר שאין צורך בו כלל.

those who study Torah also have the same two levels. To the extent that a person increases his effort in the internal aspect of Torah and its secrets, that is the extent to which Israel, the internal aspect of the world, ascends above and beyond the external elements, the nations of the world. The other nations will [then] admit and recognize the greatness of Israel, until they fulfill the verse, "They will take of those peoples and bring them into their place, and the House of Israel will possess them on the Lord's own land, slaves and bondswomen. They will be captors to their captors and rule over those who oppressed them" (Is. 14:2). Similarly, the verse states, "So says the Lord God: Behold, I shall raise My hands to nations, lift My banner toward peoples; they will bring your sons back in the folds of their robes, bearing your daughters upon their shoulders" (Is. 49:22).

Yet, God forbid, the opposite could occur. A Jewish person could demean the internal aspect of Torah and its secrets, which address the structure of our souls and their levels, as well as the role of the intellect and the reasons for mitzvot. Instead, he could focus on the external aspect of Torah, which deals only with the practical. Even if he sporadically focuses on the internal aspect, he gives it little attention, [studying it only] at a time that is neither day nor night and treating it as if it something he does not need. In that case, he will be a factor in demeaning and lowering the internal aspect of the world, the people of Israel, and he will increase the external aspect of the world, the other nations. He will lower and humiliate the people of Israel and treat Israel as if it were something unnecessary in the world, something the world does not want, God forbid.

Moreover, that person will cause the external aspect of the nations to overcome their own internal aspect. The worst among the other nations, those who cause damage and destroy the world, may become stronger and ascend above the internal aspect, the righteous among the gentiles, leading to all of the destruction and corruption witnessed by our generation (may God protect us). In that sense, the redemption of Israel and its level depends upon the study of the Zohar and the internal aspect of Torah. And the destruction and the descent of Israel occurs due to the abandonment of the internal aspect of Torah and its regard being brought down, until it was made out to be something that no one had any need for (God forbid).

ע׳

וזה שאמרו בתיקונים (תיקוני זהר תיקון ל, נתיב תניינא) וז״ל: קוּמוּ וְאִתְעָרוּ לְגַבֵּי שְׁכִינְתָּא, דְּאִית לְכוֹן לִבָּא בְּלָא סָכְלְתָנוּ לְמִנְדַּע בָּהּ, וְאִיהִי בֵּינַיְכוּ. קומו והתעוררו בשביל השכינה הקדושה, שהרי יש לכם לב ריקן בלי בינה לדעת ולהשיג אותה, אע״פ שהיא בתוככם.

וְהָא דְּמִלָּה, קוֹל אוֹמֵר קְרָא - כְּגוֹן ״קְרָא נָא הֲיֵשׁ עוֹנֶךָ, וְאֶל מִי מִקְּדוֹשִׁים תִּפְנֶה״. וְהִיא אָמְרַת: מָה אֶקְרָא, כָּל הַבָּשָׂר חָצִיר - כֻּלָּא אִינוּן כִּבְעִירָן דְּאָכְלִין חָצִיר. וְכָל חַסְדּוֹ כְּצִיץ הַשָּׂדֶה - כָּל חֶסֶד דְּעָבְדִין, לְגַרְמַיְיהוּ עָבְדִין. וסוד הדבר, כמ״ש (ישעיה מ, ו): ״קול אומר קרא״, שקול דופק בלבו של כל אחד ואחד מישראל לקרוא ולהתפלל להרמת השכינה הקדושה, שהיא כללות הנשמות של כל ישראל (ומביא ראיה מהכתוב ״קרא נא היש עונך״, שקריאה פירושה תפילה). אבל השכינה אומרת ״מה אקרא״, כלומר אין בי כוח להרים את עצמי מעפר. בשביל ש״כל הבשר חציר״, כולם המה כבהמות אוכלי עשב וחציר, כלומר שעושים המצוות בלי דעת כמו בהמות. ״וכל חסדו כציץ השדה״, כל החסדים שעושים, לעצמם הם עושים. כלומר שאין כוונתם במצוות שעושים, שתהיינה בכדי להשפיע נחת רוח ליוצרם, אלא רק לתועלת עצמם הם עושים המצוות.

וַאֲפִילוּ כָּל אִינוּן דְּמִשְׁתַּדְּלִין בְּאוֹרַיְיתָא, כָּל חֶסֶד דְּעָבְדִין לְגַרְמַיְיהוּ עָבְדִין. ואפילו הטובים שבהם שמסרו זמנם על עסק התורה, לא עשו זה אלא לתועלת גופם עצמם, בלי כוונה הרצויה בכדי להשפיע נחת רוח ליוצרם.

בְּהַהוּא זִמְנָא וכו׳ ״רוּחַ הוֹלֵךְ וְלֹא יָשׁוּב״ לְעָלְמָא, וְדָא אִיהוּ רוּחָא דְּמָשִׁיחַ. בעת ההיא, נאמר על הדור (תהלים עח, לט): ״רוח הולך ולא ישוב״ להעולם, דהיינו רוח המשיח, הצריך לגאול את ישראל מכל צרותיהם עד לגאולה השלמה, לקיים הכתוב ״ומלאה הארץ דעה את ה׳״ וגו׳ - הרוח הזה נסתלק לו והלך, ואינו מאיר בעולם.

וַי לוֹן מַאן דְּגָרְמִין דְּיֵיזִיל לֵיהּ מִן עָלְמָא וְלָא יְתוּב לְעָלְמָא, דְּאִלֵּין אִינוּן דְּעָבְדִין לְאוֹרַיְיתָא יַבֵּשָׁה וְלָא בָּעָאן לְאִשְׁתַּדְּלָא בְּחָכְמָה דְּקַבָּלָה. אוי להם לאותם אנשים הגורמים שרוחו של משיח יסתלק וילך לו מהעולם, ולא יוכל לשוב לעולם. שהמה הם העושים את התורה ליבשה, כלומר בלי משהו לחלוחית של שֵׂכל ודעת. כי מצטמצמים רק בחלק המעשי של התורה, ואינם רוצים להשתדל ולהבין בחכמת הקבלה, לידע ולהשכיל בסודות התורה וטעמי מצוה.

70

Tikkunei Zohar explains (*Tikkun* 30, *Netiv Tanina*):

> Wake and arise for the sake of the holy *Shekhina*, for you have an empty heart, devoid of understanding. You cannot acquire her [the *Shekhina*], even though she is within you…. The secret of the matter is like the verse, "A voice speaks: 'Call out!'" (Is. 40:6). It means that a voice echoes in every Jew, calling him to pray for the holy *Shekhina* to arise, for she contains all of the souls of Israel. [The Zohar brings proof from another verse that the word "call" refers to prayer.] But the *Shekhina* says, "What shall I call?" meaning, I have not the strength to lift myself up from the dust, since "Life is nothing more than grass." That means that people become like animals that eat grass; they perform mitzvot unthinkingly, like animals. "While its love [is like] green shoots upon the land." This means that people do acts of kindness only for themselves. When they perform mitzvot, they do not have intention to grant satisfaction to their Creator, but only for their own benefit. Even the best ones, who dedicate their time to involvement in Torah, do so only for their own betterment, without the proper intention to grant satisfaction to their Creator.
>
> At that time, during that generation, there will be "a passing spirit that never returns" (Ps. 78:39). This refers to the spirit of the Messiah, who needs to redeem Israel from all of their troubles, leading to the complete redemption, as the verse states, "Knowledge of the Lord will fill the earth" (Is. 11:9). This spirit has left and abandoned the world; it does not provide light.
>
> Woe unto them who cause the spirit of the Messiah to leave the world, such that it cannot ever return. They turn the Torah into a desert, without any moisture of intellect and knowledge. They limit themselves to the practical aspects of Torah, making no effort to understand the wisdom of Kabbala, to comprehend and understand the secrets of the Torah and the reasons for the commandments.

וַי לוֹן דְּגָרְמִין עֲנִיּוּתָא וְחַרְבָּא וּבִזָּה וְהֶרֶג וְאַבְדָן בְּעָלְמָא. אוי להם, שהם גורמים במעשיהם הללו, שיהיו עניות וחרב וחמס וביזה והריגות והשמדות בעולם. עכ״ל.

ע״א

וטעם דבריהם הוא כמו שבארנו, שבהיות כל עוסקי התורה מזלזלים בפנימיות שלהם ובפנימיות התורה, ומניחים אותה כמו דבר שאין צורך בו בעולם, ויעסקו בה רק בשעה שלא יום ולא לילה, והמה בה כעוורים מגששים קיר. שבזה המה מגבירים את חיצוניותם עצמם, דהיינו תועלת גופם, וכן את חיצוניות התורה המה מחשיבים על פנימיות התורה. ואז המה גורמים במעשיהם הללו, שכל בחינות החיצוניות שישנן בעולם מגבירות את עצמן על כל חלקי הפנימיות שבעולם, כל אחת לפי מהותה.

כי החיצוניות שבכלל ישראל, דהיינו עמי הארצות שבהם, מתגברת ומבטלת את הפנימיות שבכלל ישראל שהם גדולי התורה. וכן החיצוניות שבאומות העולם, שהם בעלי החורבן שבהם, מתגברת ומבטלת את הפנימיות שבהם, שהם חסידי אומות העולם. וכן חיצוניות כללות העולם, שהם אוה״ע מתגברת ומבטלת את בני ישראל, שהם פנימיות העולם. ובדור כזה, כל בעלי החורבן שבאומות העולם מרימים ראש, ורוצים בעיקר להשמיד ולהרוג את בני ישראל, דהיינו כמו שאמרו ז״ל (יבמות סג, א) ״אין פורענות באה לעולם אלא בשביל ישראל״. דהיינו כמ״ש בתיקונים הנ״ל שהם גורמים עניות וחרב ושוד והריגות והשמדות בעולם כולו.

ואחר שבעוונותינו הרבים נעשינו עדי ראיה לכל האמור בתיקונים הנ״ל. ולא עוד אלא שמידת הדין פגעה דווקא בהטובים שבנו, כמ״ש ז״ל (ב״ק ס, א) ״ואינה מתחלת אלא מן הצדיקים תחילה״. ומכל הפאר שהיה לכלל ישראל בארצות פולין וליטא וכו׳, לא נשאר לנו אלא השרידים שבארצנו הקדושה. הנה

> Woe unto them, for their actions cause the world to be poor, to be destroyed by sword; [they cause] corruption, theft, death, and destruction.

71

The explanation of the above passage in *Tikkunei Zohar* follows from what we stated above. Since all those involved in Torah denigrate their own internal aspect and the internal aspect of Torah, abandoning the [internal aspect of Torah] as if it is something that no one in the world wants and involving themselves in it only at a time that is neither night nor day, they are like a blind person feeling his way around a wall. In this way, they increase their own external aspect, meaning they benefit their bodies, as well as the external aspect of Torah, which they prefer to the internal aspect. This causes all of the external aspects of world to be strengthened, at the expense of the internal aspects, each category following its essence.

[Under these circumstances,] the external element within the people of Israel –the ignorant Jews – become stronger and overwhelm the internal element in Israel, the great Torah scholars. Similarly, the external aspect of the other nations – their destructive sides – become stronger and overwhelm the internal elements, the righteous among the gentiles. And similarly, the external elements of the entire world – the nations of the world – become stronger and overwhelm the people of Israel, who are the internal aspect of the world. In a generation such as this one, all of the destructive elements among the nations lift their heads, and they desire primarily to destroy and kill the people of Israel, as the Sages said: "Calamity befalls the world only due to the Jewish people" (Yevamot 63a). As the *Tikkunei Zohar* explains above, [those calamities] include poverty, sword, theft, death, and mass murder in the entire world.

Due to our many sins, we have witnessed everything described in that passage in *Tikkunei Zohar*. The divine attribute of justice has attacked our best, as the Sages state: "[Calamity befalls the world only when wicked people are in the world], but the [calamity] begins only with the righteous first." All of the glory of the people of Israel in Poland and Lithuania has been reduced to a handful of refugees in the Holy

מעתה מוטל רק עלינו, שארית הפליטה, לתקן את המעוות החמור הזה, וכל אחד ואחד מאתנו שרידי הפליטה, יקבל על עצמו בכל נפשו ומאודו, להגביר מכאן ואילך את פנימיות התורה וליתן לה את מקומה הראוי, כחשיבותה על מעלת חיצוניות התורה – ואז יזכה כל אחד ואחד מאתנו להגביר מעלת פנימיותו עצמו, דהיינו בחינת ישראל שבו, שהיא צרכי הנפש, על בחינת חיצוניותו עצמו, שהיא בחינת אוה״ע שבו, שהיא צרכי הגוף.

ויגיע כוח הזה גם על כלל ישראל כולו, עד שעמי הארצות שבנו יכירו וידעו את השבח והמעלה של גדולי ישראל עליהם וישמעו אליהם ויצייתו להם. וכן פנימיות אוה״ע, שהם חסידי אומות העולם, יתגברו ויכניעו את החיצוניות שלהם, שהם בעלי החורבן. וכן פנימיות העולם שהם ישראל, יתגברו בכל שבחם ומעלתם על חיצוניות העולם שהם האומות.

אז כל אומות העולם יכירו ויודו במעלת ישראל עליהם. ויקיימו הכתוב ״ולקחום עמים והביאום אל מקומם, והתנחלום בית ישראל על אדמת ה׳״ וגו׳. וכן ״והביאו בניך בחצן ובנותיך על כתף תנשאנה״. וזה שאמרו בזוהר נשא (אות צ׳) וז״ל: בְּהַאי חִבּוּרָא דִּילָךְ דְּאִיהוּ סֵפֶר הַזֹּהַר וכו׳ יִפְקוּן בֵּיהּ מִן גָּלוּתָא בְּרַחֲמֵי (בחיבור הזה שלך, של רשב״י, שהוא ספר הזוהר, יצאו בו מן הגלות ברחמים), דהיינו כמבואר. אמן כן יהי רצון.

Land. We, those who remain, must now repair the horribly distorted situation. Each and every one who remains must commit his entire being to increasing [the study] of the internal aspect of Torah and granting it its rightful place. For that is more important than the external aspect of Torah. Each and every one of us will be worthy of increasing the level of his own internal aspect, i.e., his Jewish aspect, his soul's needs. Those will become greater than his external aspect, the aspect of the "other nations," the needs of the body.

All of this energy will spread to all of Israel, to the point that even the unlearned will recognize and understand the greatness of the Torah sages, and they will listen to them and follow them. Similarly, the internal aspect of the other nations – the righteous among the gentiles – will become stronger and overcome the external aspect, the destructive forces. Similarly, the internal aspect of the world – Israel – will become stronger and greater than the external aspect of the world, the other nations.

Then, all the nations of the world will recognize and admit regarding the greatness of Israel over them. They will fulfill the verse, "They [the nations] will bring your sons back in the folds of their robes, bearing your daughters upon their shoulders" (Is. 49:22). The Zohar (*Naso* 90) explains: "This work of yours, of Rabbi Shimon bar Yoḥai – that is, the Zohar – will bring them out of the exile in mercy," as I have explained. May that be God's will.

Maggid Books
The best of contemporary Jewish thought
from Koren Jerusalem